The Cinema of Marguerite Duras

Visionaries: Thinking Through Female Filmmakers

Series Editors Lucy Bolton and Richard Rushton

Titles in the series include:

The Cinema of Marguerite Duras: Multisensoriality and Female Subjectivity
Michelle Royer

Ana Kokkinos: An Oeuvre of Outsiders
Kelly McWilliam

Habiba Djahnine: Memory Bearer
Sheila Petty

edinburghuniversitypress.com/series/vision

The Cinema of Marguerite Duras

Multisensoriality and Female Subjectivity

Michelle Royer

EDINBURGH
University Press

Edinburgh University Press is one of the leading university presses in the UK. We publish academic books and journals in our selected subject areas across the humanities and social sciences, combining cutting-edge scholarship with high editorial and production values to produce academic works of lasting importance. For more information visit our website: edinburghuniversitypress.com

We are committed to making research available to a wide audience and are pleased to be publishing Platinum Open Access editions of the ebooks in this series.

Edinburgh University Press Ltd
The Tun – Holyrood Road
12 (2f) Jackson's Entry
Edinburgh EH8 8PJ

First published in hardback by Edinburgh University Press 2019

Typeset in 12/14 Arno and Myriad by
IDSUK (Dataconnection) Ltd,
and printed and bound by CPI Group (UK) Ltd,
Croydon CRO 4YY

A CIP record for this book is available from the British Library

ISBN 978 1 4744 4054 7 (hardback)
ISBN 978 1 4744 2785 2 (paperback)
ISBN 978 1 4744 2786 9 (webready PDF)
ISBN 978 1 4744 2787 6 (epub)

Contents

Figures

Acknowledgements

My sincere thanks go to to my colleagues at the SIMD (Société Internationale Marguerite Duras) for their dedication to Duras studies, and the convening of many conferences around the world which have provided me with many opportunities to discuss and share my work.

I am grateful to the School of Languages and Cultures and the Faculty of Arts and Social Sciences at the University of Sydney for providing funding throughout my research to organise conferences and assistance with editing for this book.

I am also extremely grateful to Dr Margaret Hennessy for her rigorous and helpful suggestions and careful editing of my final draft, and to Dr Andrea Bandhauer for our many discussions on multisensoriality and neuroscience.

Lastly, I thank Simon Guthrie for his unwavering and limitless support, and Alexandra for her patient listening and suggestions.

Introduction

I am not yet up to what I have found in cinema. I will be dead when one finds why it is so powerful. As long as I make films, as long as I live, I must ignore it, I ignore it.[1] (Duras 2014b: 937)

Wherever and however we locate ourselves in the theatrical space (straight on, obscenely, or obliquely), whether blind or not to the images on screen and pervaded by sound, we are intensely attentive to the heightened sense of our own material being – to the film's resonance in or flesh, blood, viscera, breath, heart rate. (Sobchack 2006: 41)

Marguerite Duras (1914–96) died over twenty years ago but has remained one of the most important French female authors of the twentieth century and an influential writer and filmmaker. Born and raised in French Indochina, her hybrid background is at the centre of her literary and filmic work. As a woman and a postcolonial writer she has attracted a great deal of attention inside and outside France among scholars specialised in feminist and postcolonial studies, and her literary work has been translated into thirty-five languages. Twenty years after her death, and to celebrate the centenary of her birth, her complete works have been released in the prestigious Gallimard series La Pléiade (2011, 2014), making available documents that were until then difficult or impossible to access. In addition, most of her films have been made available on DVD. This represents a timely opportunity to reassess Marguerite Duras' cinema and to analyse the innovations she brought to film as she attempted to express a different vision of the world through sound and images, and from the perspective of a woman with a hybrid background.

Duras was not only a well-known writer; she was and still is considered one of the great innovators of twentieth-century literature and cinema. Her films are not as widely known as her writing, although she directed nineteen films between 1966 and 1984 and several of her novels have been adapted to the screen by reputed filmmakers. Her films, even more so than her novels, have been criticised for being too abstract and intellectual, accessible only to a select group of initiates. Because of their disruption of film conventions and their experimental exploration of the medium, they have stayed in the art-house film circuit, which has limited their access to a small, educated audience. Alison Butler believes that this inevitably limits the political effectiveness of the films and their artistic inclusiveness (Butler 2002: 8). However, I would argue that Duras' films have had an impact on cinema and spectators far beyond the immediate audience they attracted. Some of her films are considered to be cult films; for example, 1980s fans are said to have spent entire weekends watching *India Song* again and again, sometimes throughout the night. Many female filmmakers such as Claire Denis, Chantal Akerman or Sally Potter have said that they have been influenced by Duras' filmic work, and artists and theatre directors across the world have pursued Duras' reflections on cinema, literature and theatre, and, more importantly, they still do.

Her films also attracted much attention among scholars, especially feminist film critics of the late 1970s and the mid-1980s, in France, the UK and the US. Their studies were informed by psychoanalysis and the work of French feminists of difference of the mid-1970s, contemporaneous with Duras' films. In the anglophone context, feminist film theory privileged a model of film spectatorship grounded in a primacy given to vision and its various Lacanian derivatives: the gaze, identification and scopophilia based on the famous article of Laura Mulvey (1975), 'Visual Pleasure and Narrative Cinema'. In France, Duras scholars had a literary and Lacanian approach and considered films as texts. But as pointed out by Kennedy, the psychoanalytical and textual approaches did not take into account 'the viscerality and vitality of film as a processual experience' (Kennedy 2000: 42).

Considering the newly available documents on and by Duras and the surge of interest in spectatorship theories of senses, in particular the sense of touch, and in the synaesthetic and kinaesthetic dimensions of cinema, as well as the current shift from the ocular to the auditory in film theory, it is timely to reassess Duras' cinema in the light of these new approaches to cinema. Laura U. Marks' books *Touch: Sensuous Theory and Multisensory Media* (2002) and *The Skin of the Film: Intercultural Cinema, Embodiment, and the Senses* (2000), which aim to explain the ways in which intercultural cinema engages the viewer bodily to convey cultural experience and memory, are of particular relevance to Duras' films. Equally important is Jennifer Barker's *The Tactile Eye: Touch and the Cinematic Experience* (2009), which explores the visceral connection between films and spectators. It argues that the experience of cinema is a sensuous exchange between film and viewer that goes beyond the visual and aural, beneath the skin of viewers, and reverberates in their body.

Taking into account the importance Duras placed on her childhood memories and on space as well as the sensorial atmosphere of her films, a study of her cinema would benefit from such approaches to the film medium. It is the aim of this book to provide a fresh analysis and a rethinking of Duras' filmic work in the light of these new theories while still being indebted to feminist scholars for the wealth of research undertaken in the 1980s about feminine subjectivity in Duras' cinema.

Duras thought the conventions of mainstream cinema, with its hierarchical divisions and oppositions between sound and image, represented the filmic equivalent of Western power and patriarchal structures that had to be totally abolished before a new, egalitarian society and culture could exist. Hence her films had to be experimental and innovatory, create new forms of expression and provide a different experience for her spectators by replacing the focus of Western cinema on the explicit and the visible with a cinema that privileges sounds and gives a larger place to viewers' imagination. Duras' films do not always represent female characters on-screen – protagonists can be just voices on the sound track – but the disruption of film conventions, including the absence of visual representation of female characters, creates a space for the exploration of what female subjectivity might be. This disruption offers alternatives to the objectification of women in mainstream cinema, which has been the main preoccupation of feminist film theory and criticism since the 1970s. In this study of Duras' films, I will explore the effect of the subversion of film conventions on the exposure of the feminine and on the film medium. I will argue that through a disruption of narratives, characterisation, synchronisation, visuality and elaborated soundscapes, Duras displaces the emphasis from film narrative to film materiality with its synaesthetic potential and proposes to spectators an immersion in the sensorial world of female subjectivity. Like Bolton in her book *Film and Female Consciousness: Irigaray, Cinema and Thinking Women* (2011), I use the term 'female' to discuss the sexed body of women, and 'feminine' to refer to the symbolic codes and representations of what is considered to be female (Bolton 2011: 3). Many times in this study, the concepts are intertwined or are found to be inseparable; however, I have been conscious of the risk of essentialism which a systematic amalgamation of the two concepts could lead to, and the issue of essentialism will be discussed in the first chapter of this book. I have opted for the use of female subjectivity in the context of Duras' work. The term 'female subjectivity' emphasises that the films are from the perspective of a particular female subject who has experienced the human condition, in Duras' case the colonial situation, the complexity of World War II, the Algerian War, the May 1968 revolution and the feminist movement, from a female viewpoint. It is these experiences that made her the female author and filmmaker she was. Her work refracts those situations at conscious and unconscious levels, and any attempt to separate the fact she was a female from the experiences she lived and the artistic expressions of these experiences would be artificial and would not do justice to her work. Gender and power relations are always present, and Duras wrote widely and gave many interviews in the media about being a female author, writer/ playwright/filmmaker. These were published in compilations such as *Les parleuses* (*Woman to Woman*), *Les Lieux de Marguerite Duras* and *Les Yeux verts* (Duras 2014c). They contain a wealth of information about Duras, her vision of the world, of literature and cinema. She often stresses that her perspective as a female author cannot be detached from the fact that she spent her childhood in colonial Indochina. Being a female writer is central to her subjectivity and so is the situation she was brought up in as a child. She was constructed by her gender and her situation as the daughter in a poor colonial family. Her family relationships, especially her relationships with her mother and brother, also structured her as a female subject. The combination of these factors constituted the ground and background on which her subjectivity was formed. The feeling of injustice (being female, not being liked by her mother, the poverty she lived in as a poor member of the colonial community) is central to her work and to her female perspective.

Equally important is the fact that she belonged to the French colonial power in Indochina.

In my previous book on the cinema of Marguerite Duras, *L'Écran de la passion* (1997), I showed that Luce Irigaray, Julia Kristeva and Hélène Cixous' reflections on the question of femininity or 'the feminine' shaped the intellectual context in which Duras approached the question of female subjectivity in her cinema. Some feminists have challenged their works for being essentialist, but interestingly, Irigaray's writing has made a return to the scene of feminist film theory. Scholars such as Caroline Bainbridge and Lucy Bolton have drawn on her work with the aim of revealing different ways of understanding female protagonists in cinema. These studies have inspired this book, although Duras' characters are never coherent, always fragmented, and are not even always visually present so such approaches, directly applied to a study of Duras' films, would not do justice to the innovations her films brought to cinema.

This book, borrowing Irigaray's approach to the feminine, will investigate how Duras' filmic innovations such as the disjunction of film and image, the primacy given to voices, silence and music, long black shots, track shots, colours, and so on, opened a sensorial space for her female inner experience to be expressed, and felt by viewers. As the film narrative conventions are peeled away, touch, smell, hearing take the centre stage, creating for spectators a powerful multisensory experience. While this book does not intend to advance the idea that film viewing as embodied, multisensory and synaesthetic experience is intrinsically linked to the exposure of the feminine, it will attempt to show that Duras' subversion of conventions of filmmaking leads spectators to experience her films from a specific and complex sensory and feminine bodily space.

The films also provide food for thought about cinema, memories, passion and loss. As explained by Laine in her recent publication *Bodies in Pain: Emotion and the Cinema of Darren Aronofsky* (2017), cinematic experience is both reflexive and aesthetic, a matter of affective participation in the filmic event, based on mutual resonance felt in the body and reflected in thought. Laine, like Antunes (2016), considers cinema as an aesthetic form that addresses our affects and senses, while as a conceptual practice it engages our thinking and imagination: the sensuous and the conceptual are intertwined (Laine 2017: 19). Films embody ideas as they embody experiences and emotions, but these ideas and emotions can only emerge through interaction with the spectator who feels and thinks with the film (Laine 2017: 19).

According to Bolton (2011: 193), Irigaray recognises the importance of art as a means of expression for women. The repression of feminine genealogies and cultures is a cause of the limitations upon women's subjectivities, and 'art remains a crucial means of expression and communication, needed for us to enter into relationships and to cultivate our sensorial perceptions through a creative imagination' (Bolton 2011: 194), which must work 'not only with words but also with colours and sounds as possible matters to represent, communicate and sublimate fleshly energy and attraction' (Irigaray 2004a: 99).

In the first chapter of this book, I will discuss the theoretical framework on which my analysis of Duras' work is based. I suggest that the impact of Duras' films on spectators can be better understood by recent spectatorship theories on multisensoriality but that gender has to be reintroduced into these theories, which have tended to present themselves as gender neutral. As is often the case, gender neutrality results in an unacknowledged masculine viewpoint. So, in this first chapter, I will examine recent works in film theory that deal with multisensoriality, reception theories and embodiment, and will connect them to feminist theories on feminine subjectivity, in particular in the work of Duras' feminist contemporaries including Julia Kristeva, Luce Irigaray and Hélène Cixous, who explored the feminine as linked to preverbal experiences and the senses. Both sets of theories, on multisensorial spectatorship and on the feminine, bear similarities and have reconfigured the cinematic and the female experience to include the participation of body and senses. I will also respond to the accusation of essentialism against these authors in support of Bainbridge's and Bolton's analyses.

Chapter 2 provides necessary biographical and historical information for the study. Duras was a woman of her time, so her life, political involvement and contemporaries are important to include as they allow us to contextualise the filmmaker and her work. The second chapter also looks at the reasons why Duras came to cinema after a long period essentially devoted to writing.

From Chapter 3, I will begin an in-depth examination of Duras' innovative techniques and filmic strategies. The best-known innovation that Duras brought to cinema is the disjunction or desynchronisation of sound and image, which will be the topic of the third chapter. The audio-visual disjunction is a device that allowed her to destabilise the conventional hierarchy between sound and image, which she saw as reproducing the power structures of society. By deconstructing cinematic strategies of representation, Duras opens her films to her sensorial world, which will be analysed in detail and linked to feminist theories.

Chapter 4 will focus on the visuality of the films, their tactility and hapticity and their effects on spectators. The introduction of the black screen will be given a special place because it brings together many aspects of Duras filmic work: desire for destruction, strong connection with art, and the privileging of the materiality of cinema at the expense of the narratives. This chapter will show how particular visual film techniques can involve spectators and lead them to experience the sensorial world of a female subject.

In the final chapter, 'Soundscape: Sonic Aesthetics and the Feminine', I will examine the role and complexity of sound and how it instils a particular experience in Duras' audiences. Chion's theories on sound and theories on the feminine will be linked and discussed.

The conclusion will highlight the characteristics of Duras' sensorial world and will consider the legacy of the filmmaking of Duras, whose work has influenced and continues to inspire filmmakers, video artists, painters and writers.

Note

1   (My translation) 'Je ne suis pas encore à la hauteur de ce que j'ai trouvé au cinéma. Je serai morte quand on aura trouvé pourquoi c'est tellement fort. Tant que je fais du cinéma, tant que je vis je dois l'ignorer, je l'ignore.'

1

Film theory, multisensoriality and the feminine

Sexual difference probably represents the most universal question we can address. Our era is faced with the task of dealing with this issue, because, across the whole world, there are, there are only, men and women. (Irigaray 1996: 47)

In the last twenty years, film spectatorship has been the object of new approaches with concepts such as spectator embodiment, simulated embodiment, hapticity, synaesthesia and multisensoriality. These concepts are based on research in phenomenology, perception theories and neuroscience, and place the body as the site of reception. If the body has always figured to some extent in film theory, dominant discourse has tended to privilege one sense, vision and its relationship to self.

In the 1970s, semiotics and psychoanalysis dominated the studies of spectatorship among Western film scholars such as Christian Metz and Jean-Louis Baudry. Retaining the psychoanalytical model, Laura Mulvey adopted a feminist approach in her famous article 'Visual Pleasure and Narrative Cinema' (1975). Mulvey argued that film only serves to perpetuate a type of male-driven patriarchal language that facilitates male visual pleasure. As a result, female spectators have no access to it other than through the male gaze that consistently objectifies female characters. For Mulvey, female spectators will be able to find true pleasure from films only by inventing a new type of film language that is not driven by narrative. The emphasis placed by Mulvey on the visual has been widely criticised for limiting the film to a visual art. However, the strategies she advocates in order to make cinema a medium that represents women have led some female filmmakers to defy narrative and film conventions. In many ways Duras' films present this very type of questioning by challenging dominant cinema, subverting the primacy of the image over the sound, the ocular over the auditory, and the notion of narrative and female character. Duras' cinema can be understood in the context of the questioning that was taking place at the time she was involved in filmmaking: the May 1968 student revolution in France, French feminism of difference and the reflection by filmmakers and gender film theorists on female spectatorship. They all have in common the desire to destroy or at least to challenge dominant power structures, although their approaches can differ significantly.

After the predominantly visual twentieth century and its semiotic and post-structuralist influence on criticism, today's film scholars seem to turn away from the image 'as readable text to the image as subjectively and bodily experiential event' (Laine and Strauven 2009: 250). Not only are scholars recognising film as an auditory as well as a visual medium, but vision is no longer thought to be 'rooted in the eye itself, but rather extends to corporeality, affect, and sensation' (Kirshtner 2005: 4–5). The insertion of the body and its feelings into film theory has its roots in Deleuze's theories on affect in cinema: the film is no longer seen simply as representing emotions to which viewers identify, but a film exists as a rhizome that connects with the senses of spectators. Rather than consider the film as simply an assemblage of signs, the concept of rhizome enables us to rethink the relationship between film and spectator. As explained by Steven Shaviro in the *Cinematic Body*:

> When I am caught up in watching a film I do not really 'identify' in the psychoanalytic sense with the activity of the (male) protagonist, or with that protagonist's gaze, or even with what theorists have called the 'omnivoyeuristic' look of the camera. It is more the case that I am brought into intimate contact with the images on screen by a process of mimesis or contagion. (Shaviro 1993: 51)

Elliott considers Shaviro's work as the first step in the evolution of theories of the body as a site of reception for film (Elliott 2011: 34). Since Shaviro's *The Cinematic Body*, much has been written about the body in film, about touch and the notion of hapticity in cinema, and these writings will inform aspects of my study, although Duras' cinema has been neglected by most of these studies.

Laura Marks has produced the most significant discussion on the phenomenological bases of multisensory perception in *The Skin of the Film* (2000), which has given rise to a range of phenomenological approaches to film including Barker's *The Tactile Eye* (2009), and Beugnet's *Cinema and Sensation: French Cinema and the Art of Transgression* (2007). Marks' study focuses on intercultural cinema and the haptic visuality of film, a visuality that functions like a sense of touch, what she calls the 'skin of the film'. Intercultural films selected by Marks are films made by exiled filmmakers who cannot physically revisit their original home culture. She explains:

> Many of these works evoke memories both individual and cultural, through an appeal to the nonvisual knowledge, embodied knowledge, and experiences of the senses, such as touch, smell, and taste. In particular, I explore ... how certain images appeal to a haptic, or tactile, visuality. (Marks 2000: 2)

Haptic images invite spectators to 'respond to the image in an intimate, embodied way, and thus facilitate the experience of other sensory impressions as well' (Marks 2000: 2). They allow exiled filmmakers to reach the material world of those unreachable home places through sensory memories and to evoke not only haptic memories but also memories of textures and scents.

This is particularly relevant to our topic because Duras was in many ways an exiled filmmaker: she lived her childhood in Vietnam and never returned to her birthplace. While her films do not narrate stories taking place in Indochina, the Indian cycle (*La femme du Gange, India Song, Son nom de Venise dans Calcutta désert*) recreates the multisensory world of an imaginary Asian colony in the 1930s. It is as if through the film medium, Duras was trying to access the traces of that multisensorial world and reproduce them by the means of the audio-visual device, while refusing to fall into a realistic and autobiographical representation.

Marks looks at a number of films that appeal to the senses of touch, smell, taste and entire environments of sense experience (Marks 2000: 22), and concludes that synaesthesia and haptic visuality enable the viewer to experience cinema as multisensory. While her study is very useful for the examination of the multisensory experience of

Duras' films, it tends to limit the film to a visual medium. She gives primacy to the image, considering that in our Western societies sound being an information medium, dialogue-centred narratives reflect this use of sound. Sound is kept at the margin of her study, although she recognises that it can be ambient and textural, and even haptic, and that music, talk, ambient sound and silence are important to the feeling of embodied experience intercultural films produce. In Duras' films the soundtrack, which is very rich and complex, will have a central place in our study.

Laura McMahon is the only scholar who has approached Duras' cinema from this contemporary perspective. In her book *Cinema and Contact: the Withdrawal of Touch in Nancy, Bresson, Duras and Denis*, she focuses on the question of community in the films of Duras 'elaborating connections between tactility and community via Nancy's thinking of co-existence' (McMahon 2012: 74). While this contribution to Duras' scholarship is very valuable, it focuses only on the sense of tactility which is analysed through the filter of Nancy's theories. My approach to Duras' films will not be limited to visual, touch and auditory senses; it will also examine the olfactory senses and three other senses which Antunes has brought to our attention: vestibular or spatial awareness, nociception or sense of pain, and thermoception.

Cinema cannot provide a direct experience or smell, taste, kinaesthesia, pain or warmth. These can only be perceived by indirect means, through sight and hearing and inferential clues. For example, Antunes asserts that: 'although our eyes cannot see and our ears cannot hear thermal energy, they can perceive sensory manifestations of temperature not only in the material world around us but also in mediated film's world' (Antunes 2016: loc. 3077)

Following Marks' and Antunes' film theories, my starting point is to consider film as providing a multisensorial experience. While in cinema, information is transmitted through an audio-visual medium, spectators perceive the film with all their senses:

> Not only *can* our brains perceive an audiovisual medium in a multisensory way, but they must do so because there is no other way for our perception to occur. Our natural, not exceptional or synesthetic, way of perceiving is multisensory. (Antunes 2016: loc. 95)

Film is an experiential art form that uses its audio-visual specificity to reach the multisensoriality of human perception, and, as explained by Bordwell, style is what shapes spectators' sensorial experience:

> However much the spectator may be engaged by plot or genre, subject matter or thematic implication, the texture of the film experience depends centrally upon the moving images and the sound that accompanies them. The audience gains access to story or theme only through that tissue of the sensory materials … However unaware spectators may be of it, style is working at every moment to shape their experience. (Bordwell 1997: 7–8)

Neuroscience has, of late, been very influential on our understanding of spectatorship. Vittorio Gallese's concept of embodied simulation based on findings of the mirror neuron system attempts to explain what is happening to spectators when they watch a film. Our brain would spontaneously simulate (or re-enact) the actions that we see others performing in front of us, including on-screen (Rizzolatti and Craighero 2004; Gallese and Guerra 2012a, 2012b). Duras' films challenge and even destroy narratives and character representations, so the question of embodied simulation in the context of her cinema will be of particular interest in our study. What spectators are often left with are pure images and sounds, and it is through them that other senses are stimulated. Our perceptual experiences resulting from audio-visual sensory information become multisensory in their final perceptual result.

Studies from phenomenologists, neuroscientists or philosophers such as Deleuze all agree that our senses do not work in isolation, but they continuously work in close and synergetic ways, or through synaesthesia. In the area of film studies, Steven Shaviro (1993), Vivian Sobchack (1992) and Laura Marks (2000) have paved the way to our understanding of synaesthesia in film with notions of embodiment, haptic and cinaesthetic subjects which replace concepts of identification and visual pleasure by notions of textures of sensual encounters between film and spectators. Synaesthesia is not an intellectual phenomenon but a perceptual experience, where all the senses are triggered. It recombines with lived experience and memory, memory being our capacity to access sensory experiences.

In their article 'The Synaesthetic Turn', Tarja Laine and Wanda Strauven show that in the last ten years, synaesthesia has had a strong impact in various fields of scientific research and artistic practice. Synaesthesia is no longer considered to be exceptional and has moved away from a clinical definition. It is defined as joined perception or mixing of the senses which is no longer addressed solely at the eye (or the visually thinking mind), but at a multisensorial or polysensorial body (Laine and Strauven 2009: 250), and which affects everyone. It is directed at the body as a whole, that is, the body as a complex, interactive and sensory apparatus. Synaesthesia has been explored in great depth by Cytowic: *Synaesthesia: a Union of the Senses* (2002), to explain the 'intuited cross-modal nature of our experience of art' (Antunes 2016: loc. 877). Today, the concept of synaesthesia pervades all possible areas, affecting not only the art world and academic research in the humanities, but also the so-called 'hard' sciences, where Antonio Damasio's motto 'I feel, therefore I am' is challenging Descartes' version of dualism (Laine and Strauven 2009: 251).

In studies on embodiment and multisensoriality, the gender question is sometimes mentioned but never given proper consideration. This is an interesting point, as the body is central to theories of perception and embodiment, but they assume a neutral body, an un-gendered and culturally non-specific body. Elliott points out that Merleau-Ponty's phenomenology, on which a number of the studies in question based themselves, makes no mention of the various physical differences that exist between men and women or the differences that exist through enculturation and sexualisation (Elliott 2011: 65).

The perceptual lived body is worth investigating in the context of feminism, partly because Duras directed films during the heyday of French feminism of difference of the 1970s, partly because several feminist theorists have asserted the value of touch and taste over sight, and shown how this challenges our notion of a fixed subjectivity.

Duras' world is the sensory world of a female subject which, as mentioned earlier, is constructed by many elements. Her experience is that of a woman perceiving and experiencing the sensory world: it cannot be divorced from her childhood in Vietnam and Cambodia, her life as poor colonialist, her experience of World War II, heterosexual love, the pain of losing a child, of losing a male lover, of being betrayed and rejected, and so on. Her multifaceted subjectivity cannot be dissociated from the fact she was a female subject experiencing life and constructing the multisensoriality of these experiences in her films.

The works of Luce Irigaray, Julia Kristeva and Hélène Cixous are mentioned in the critical theory and embodiment chapter of Paul Elliott's book. He stresses the importance of being aware of these feminist theories while discussing embodiment and multisensory theories because they question the primacy of vision which would be due 'not to some innate originary relationship between what we see and who we are, but to the proliferation of masculine modes of being' and therefore are 'vital to a study ... that is based on the hypothesis that technology such as cinema relies on senses other than optical sight for its impact' (Elliott 2011: 67), but he does not develop this.

Irigaray's work has recently enjoyed a renaissance, with new translations appearing in English and several monographs 'sketching the on-going interest in the politics and philosophy of the feminine' (Bainbridge 2008: 1). Although Irigaray's work became widely known and influential among scholars specialised in gender studies in the 1980s, it was criticised by feminists for being essentialist and as a result ceased to be used in film and literary criticism. However, Irigaray's theories on the feminine have regained the interest of film scholars, and the accusation of essentialism is now challenged and thought to be a misreading of her work. As suggested by Bainbridge:

> The critique of essentialism in Irigaray's work does not take into account the very radical attempts made throughout her work to posit a critique of patriarchy that makes possible a mode of change that has ramifications for notions of gendered subjectivity. In claiming that Irigaray's work is ahistorical and non-materialist, such accounts reveal the extent to which Irigaray's work has been dismissed on the basis of misreadings of her earlier texts. (Bainbridge 2008: 8)

Bainbridge (2008: 8) quotes Schor who suggests that 'Irigaray is not interested in defining "woman", but is rather committed to *theorizing* feminine specificity in terms that give due consideration to questions of sexual difference' (Burke et al. 1994: 66).

Some now perceive a connection between the new spectatorship theories based on phenomenology, Deleuze's theories on the haptic and affect, and Irigaray's idea of the necessity of creating a space for female subjectivity and the feminine (for example, Bolton 2011, Chamarette 2015 and, to some extent, Elliott 2011).

Irigaray makes a link between gender and vision in *Speculum of the Other Woman* (1985a), pointing out that Freudian sexual theories on the penis envy and woman as lacking rely heavily on the importance of seeing. They ignore other senses, such as touch and smell, which she demonstrates are intrinsic to women's sexuality.

Bainbridge argues that Irigaray's work is relevant to film because cinema, unlike literary texts, does not privilege the written/logocentric and visual senses alone: 'Cinema does not depend solely on its visuality: other diegetic factors such as the soundtrack, the editing/camera-positioning and the way diegetic time and space are represented also contribute to the construction of a film's textuality' (Bainbridge 2008: 12).

Irigaray's theories will be useful to understand female subjectivity in the films of Duras, as they undoubtedly resonate with Duras' innovative strategies of film representations. As explained by Bainbridge, the cinematic text follows other texts, such as the screenplay or, in the case of Duras the novel or the play, becomes a non-linear and a non-logocentric text that has the potential to rework the symbolic patterns of representations of the feminine. This is an interesting thought when applied to Duras' work, because she came to cinema after a successful career as a writer. Her written texts do not follow the conventions of genre and of narrative. In fact, Duras saw her writing process as one of destruction of literary conventions. With cinema, she attempted to go even further in the destruction of narrative conventions as she thought making a film destroys the original text. She writes: 'To destroy what is written and thus does not end, I have to make a film from the book' (quoted and translated by Borgomano 2009: 66). These transgressive, innovative strategies create new spaces and interstices where something else can be heard. Irigaray's notion of the feminine and her emphasis on questions of space, time and the female voice will be helpful as they will allow us to link the subversive filmic strategies used by Duras to the feminine and multisensoriality. Whilst Irigaray is not proposing a definition of women and the feminine, she recognises that in a patriarchal context, women are unable to conceive of their difference. She suggests a number of strategies for women to challenge patriarchal order and to think about themselves differently. Female filmmakers can produce something different with female subjectivity. As explained by Bolton: 'they create space for the female characters to explore themselves and others, using language, the body and consciousness, offering a vision of a possible alternative way of being for women in cinema' (Bolton 2011: 10). Female characters are, however, fictional constructions of femininity, whereas the entire film as an audio-visual medium is the product of a female subject (although the question of film authorship will be nuanced in a later chapter). Hence, I contend that female subjectivity should be studied not solely through the representation of female characters, but also through the filmic innovations that create the multisensoriality of films.

The argument developed in this book is that Duras created a multisensory world in her films, but she had to disrupt filmic conventions for her female sensorial experience to be expressed and exposed. This is not to say that all women would perceive and express their sensorial world in the same fashion, but the gender element cannot be excluded from subjectivity and multisensoriality as it permeates every experience. In order to represent her experience, Duras had to break conventions for many reasons – political, personal, contextual and sexual – as they were constructed predominantly by men of a certain class who dominated the industry and basically reflected men's perception of the world and patriarchal discourse.

On the side of reception, spectators, male or female, perceive films through their senses, but the films they perceive reconstitute a female or male sensorial experience of the world. As suggested by Marks:

> The cinematic encounter takes place not only between my body and the film's body, but my sensorium and the film's sensorium. We bring our own personal and cultural organisation of the senses to cinema, and cinema brings a particular organisation of the senses to us, the filmmaker's own sensorium refracted through the cinematic apparatus. (Marks 2000: 152–3)

The encounter between the sensorium of Duras' films and the spectators' bodies will be the focus of this book, but we will always underline that gender permeates this encounter at the site of the film and at the experience of its reception. However, first of all we need to discuss the question of film authorship, since throughout this first chapter we have considered Duras the auteur of her films. The notion of the filmmaker as auteur has been challenged by many scholars, so we will begin our study by examining the way Duras has inscribed authorship in her films. It will provide a strong justification for studying her films as the refraction of her sensorium.

2

Inscribing authorship

Pendant dix ans elle avait eu envie d'aller au cinéma et elle n'avait pu y aller qu'une fois en se cachant. Pendant dix ans cette envie était restée en elle aussi fraîche, tandis qu'elle, elle vieillissait. (Duras 1950: 283–4)

A film is an act of seeing that makes itself seen, an act of hearing that makes itself heard, an act of physical and reflexive movement that makes itself reflexively felt and understood. (Sobchack 1992: 37)

Biographical information

Marguerite Duras was a very prolific writer before she became a filmmaker. She produced over twenty novels, nearly as many plays, and between 1966 and 1985 she directed a total of nineteen films. She also published a great number of essays and journalistic articles, and gave many press, television and radio interviews where she recalled her early life in Indochina, and her relationship with her mother and brothers. All these texts and films intertwine, making classification difficult and the separation between facts and fiction even more arduous.

In her article 'The Duras Phenomenon', written a year after Duras' death, Margaret Sankey explored the extraordinary relationship Duras enjoyed with her French readers and her critics, concluding: 'No other woman writer in contemporary times in France has provoked such extreme emotions. She is, it seems, either loved or despised. Her capacity for provoking "le scandale" is legendary' (Sankey 1997: 60).

Such was Duras' reputation while alive. Since her death in 1996, her work and her persona have continued to attract interest from readers, spectators, scholars and critics. In France and outside of the French-speaking world, Marguerite Duras is now considered to be a key figure of French literature and cinema. Her complete works have been published in the prestigious series La Pléiade (Gallimard), a guarantee of her place in the history of French literature and cinema.

Duras has been the subject of nine biographies, so there is ample information about her life, although Duras specialists, influenced by 1960s French criticism and Roland Barthes' work, wanted to dissociate literary production from the author's existence; they were very cautious when it came to analysing her fictional texts in the light of her life. Furthermore, they were acutely aware of the uncertainty of her life story, with the mixture of concealment, distortion and revelation contained in her autobiographical accounts, from *Un barrage contre le Pacifique* (1950) to *L'Amant de la Chine du nord* (1991). Therefore, most biographical accounts have been confined to journalists or non-academic researchers (Frédérique Lebelley, Laure Adler, Jean Vallier). Journalist Laure Adler's *Marguerite Duras*, published in France in 1998, immediately became a bestseller, winning the Goncourt Prize for autobiography and propelling Duras into the headlines. However, the most rigorous and detailed biography is considered to be Jean Vallier's two-volume *C'était Marguerite Duras* (2006, 2010).

As mentioned earlier, Duras' life, writing and cinema are all intertwined, and biographical events can no longer be ignored in any study of her work, although they have to be selected with care. I will attempt to provide a brief account of Duras' life to assist readers of this book with the biographical details to which I will refer throughout this study.

Marguerite Donnadieu (Duras is a pseudonym) was born in the French colony of Indochina in 1914 of French parents who were both teachers. The only girl in the family, she had two older brothers. Her father died when she was only seven. The three children were brought up in Indochina by their single mother who never remarried. Her father originated from a village in the Périgord region called Duras, where the young girl spent two years after her father's death. She had such fond memories of the place she decided to use its name as a pseudonym, although, interestingly, the figure of the father appears rarely in her autobiographical writings, her interviews, her fiction and her films, and it is clear that Duras' imagination is firmly located within a female universe.

After the death of the father, Duras' family lived in relative poverty on the mother's income. They were marginalised by the white colonial community because of their social status: they were poor, and the mother was bringing up her children alone. This had a strong impact on Duras' life as she always saw herself as an outsider. In her novel *Un barrage contre le Pacifique* (1950) she revealed these feelings of alienation through the character of Suzanne. In her autobiographical writings and interviews, she often described how her mother bought land in Cambodia and attempted to build a wall to protect her rice fields, but it was destroyed by the tides of the Pacific Ocean. Subsequently, the family had to return to Saigon where the mother suffered a breakdown. Duras had a very strong, visceral attachment to her mother throughout her life, although she felt quite ambivalent about her. The victim of violence from her mother and one of her brothers, she suffered immensely from her mother's rejection.

After finishing her baccalaureate in the Vietnamese language at the age of eighteen, Duras embarked for Paris to begin university studies. She would never return to Indochina. In 1939 she married Robert Antelme, who was later arrested and deported to Dachau concentration camp. Helped by François Mitterrand, he was able return to France, but Duras' discovery of the atrocities of the camps had a profound impact on her writing and filmmaking. The Holocaust and the Jewish exile are at the centre of several of her works, such as *La Douleur, Aurélia Steiner (Melbourne)* and *Aurélia Steiner (Vancouver).*

After the war, she joined the French Communist Party with Robert Antelme, and was a very committed member. However, she was unable to accept the party's loyalty to Stalinism and was officially expelled, like many other intellectuals for being 'deviationist'. *Le Camion* (1977), Duras' most political film, is a reflection on this period of her life and is about the deep disappointment she felt when she was excluded from the party after seven years as a devoted member. In her text presenting the film to the press, she expresses the feeling of loss of hope: 'There is no need any more to play the game of socialist hope. Of capitalist hope. Not worth pretending there is justice to come, whether it is social, fiscal or otherwise'[1] (Duras 2014a: 303). Despite this, she continued to call herself a communist until the end of her life, confiding to Laure Adler: 'The communist hope never left me. Hope was my sickness, hope in the proletariat' (Adler 2001: 179).

Duras had begun to write novels in the 1940s, beginning with *Les Impudents* (1943), and almost won the Goncourt Prize in 1950 with *Un barrage contre le Pacifique*. Her first novels all presented a linear narrative, but her writing style changed with *Moderato Cantabile* (1958) when it became less conventional, perhaps under the influence of the *nouveau roman*. With *Le Ravissement de Lol V. Stein* (1964) she was truly 'recognized as a writer with a distinctive voice, talking of love, pain and loss, and slightly exotic because of her Vietnamese childhood' (Sankey 1997: 62).

She took political stands throughout her life, and during the Algerian War of Independence (1954), alongside other intellectuals such as Sartre and Beauvoir, she protested against the torture of Algerian prisoners and the atrocities committed by the French Army. She wrote several newspaper articles showing her concerns about racism against Algerians in France. Given Duras' childhood in the colonies, her 'strong reaction in this context may well have been triggered by her earlier experience of colonial oppression in Indochina' (Günther 2002: 10). In her cinema, her representations of India under British rule in *India Song* (1975) and of the exploitation of immigrant workers in France in *Les Mains négatives* (1979) express similar concerns.

Duras was an active participant in the May revolution of 1968 and this was in keeping with her communist and anti-colonialist engagement. She was a fervent opponent of the authoritarian French president de Gaulle, and the 'May 68' movement, with its anti-establishment position, its refusal of hierarchies and its anarchic spontaneity, matched her philosophy. This period inaugurated her work as a filmmaker. Her film *Détruire dit-elle* (1969) was directly inspired by the May 1968 events and made her known outside of France. As the title suggests, her aim was to break down Western power structures, social hierarchies and narrative conventions. It also shows that for Duras, it is only out of the destruction of the old world that a new communist, egalitarian society will rise.

Until then, Duras had been perceived as a marginal left-wing writer, but throughout the 1970s her image changed, and she began to be seen as a feminist writer. She supported the MLF (Mouvement de libération des femmes/Women's Liberation Movement), contributed to feminist magazines and signed pro-abortion manifestos. Her work became strongly influenced by feminist ideas, although she maintained an ambivalent attitude towards feminist groups, as she was distrustful of French political movements since her disappointment with the Communist Party. Günther explains that 'having spent her childhood and adolescence in Vietnam, she often expresses a feeling of alienation from any concept of French identity and a sense of not quite belonging to France' (Günther 2001: 13).

In 1974, she published a series of interviews with Xavière Gauthier, *Les Parleuses* (*Woman to Woman* 1987) set in the framework of French feminism of difference, as a result of which her work became the object of many analyses by French, British and American feminist scholars using psychoanalytical gender theories. Marcelle Marini (1977) published a powerful interpretation of Duras' writing in which she saw the representation of oppressed and excluded feminine desire, while *Camera Obscura*, a North American journal of feminism, culture and media studies, published several important articles on Duras' cinema during the 1980s. Many PhD theses on Duras' work were also written at that time.

Duras' interest in and contribution to cinema began with her collaboration with Alain Resnais on the film *Hiroshima mon amour* (1959). She wrote the script and actively contributed to the film, but she waited almost ten years before directing her first film. Between 1967 and 1984 she made seventeen films and wrote many scripts, but during that time she published only a few works of fiction. However, in 1984 she won the Goncourt Prize with her autobiographical novel *L'Amant* which became an instant bestseller. After the success of *L'Amant*, she made only one film, *Les Enfants* (1985).

With the publication of *L'Amant*, her work, which had been considered to be so subversive and difficult, was finally accessible to everyone, partly because of its relationship to her life. *L'Amant* was translated into twenty-nine languages and projected her onto the national and international media stage: 'She became a media star whose opinion was sought frequently and who was constantly under scrutiny' (Sankey 1997: 65). The woman Duras became more important than her writing: 'For Duras's French critics, after *L'Amant*, Duras's life and work are mingled inextricably and the behaviour of the woman is ascribed more importance than that of her writing, which is colonized, backgrounded, categorized and put aside' (Sankey 1997: 66).

Jean-Jacques Annaud's film adaptation of the book was released in 1992. At first it was a collaborative effort with Duras, but irreconcilable differences made her leave the project. Annaud's *L'Amant* was the most expensive film ever made in France and his attempts to represent the sexual desire of the female protagonist evoked in the novel made the film almost pornographic. It was a great commercial success, but it did not do justice to the novel as it failed to respect the anti-conventional, subtle, understated aesthetics of the text (Günther 2002: 136). It made a Hollywood story out of Duras' unconventional autobiographical novel.

Throughout her life, Duras had passionate love affairs, which she revealed in her autobiographies, and had one child with Dionys Mascolo. In *Woman to Woman* and *Les Lieux de Marguerite Duras* she discussed the importance of motherhood in her life and her incredible devotion to her son, which would also have a strong impact on her films.

In the last part of her life she lived with a young man, Yann Andréa, who became an inspiration for her work. He appears in her films *Agatha et les lectures illimitées* (1981), *L'Homme atlantique* (1981) and *Il Dialoguo di Roma* (1982), and is evoked in several of her novels, such as *Yann Andréa Steiner* (1992). His inclusion in her filmic work has contributed to what I call the filmic performance of authorship.

Coming to cinema

As mentioned earlier, by the time Duras embarked on her career as a film director in the 1960s, not only was she a well-known and acclaimed author but one for whom cinema had been an important presence in her life and her writing.

Duras liked to say that what motivated her to direct her own films was her disappointment with the adaptations of her novels to the screen. She strongly disliked René Clément's *Un barrage contre le Pacifique* (1958), Peter Brook's *Moderato Cantabile* (1960), Jules Dassin's *Dix heures et demie du soir en été* (1966) and Tony Richardson's *Le Marin de Gibraltar* (1967). They followed realistic models of representation, which she thought betrayed her work. She felt she was the only one who could adequately direct her films, conveying the internal world of her characters and their reactions to the world.

Although she devoted herself essentially to writing until 1960, cinema was already an important theme in her novel *Un barrage contre le Pacifique* (1950). According to the Duras scholar Madeleine Borgomano, long before she began making films, 'Duras was immersed in the fascinating effects of cinema, which she linked to her childhood and adolescence. She integrated these experiences into her fiction, anticipating the direction she would much later pursue' (Borgomano 2009: 83). Cinema and the character of the Mother are closely intertwined in *The Sea Wall* (the English translation of *Un barrage contre le Pacifique*) as the Mother was a piano player at a silent movie theatre called The Eden. She played for hours below the level of the screen while the children slept on benches. According to Borgomano, cinema is part of the powerful and painful spells of Duras' occulted childhood, lately intruding and triumphing over oblivion. What Duras did through filmmaking was 'to put into cinematic form the magic whose germs were already contained in her childhood' (Borgomano 2009: 69).

If cinema is linked to childhood memories, Duras' literary style in *Moderato Cantabile* made her conversion to cinema a natural progression, according to Günther: 'The sparsity of descriptive detail and the shift from narration to dialogue facilitated her gradual move to the cinema' (Günther 2002: 14). However, another important factor that contributed to her active involvement in cinema is the impact that writing was having on her life. She felt that writing was dangerous, and she even feared it could lead her to madness because of the solitude that was necessary for her to write. Filmmaking involved working in a team that, for her, was less dangerous than writing. But after ten years making films, she returned to writing: 'I was going to write books again, to return to my native land, to that terrifying work left behind ten years before' (quoted and translated by McMahon 2012: 97).

For Borgomano, Duras' systematic destruction of writing and of the novel format left no way for the author to go on writing and, after *Amour* (1972), 'a daring attempt to reach the limits of writing' (Borgomano 2009: 65), she devoted herself to cinema. Duras perceived cinema as the continuation of the process of destruction of writing as she aimed at the destruction of her characters, and of writing itself. Paradoxically, her conversion to filmmaking offered her not only a burst of creativity, but it also allowed movement, sound, light and colour to re-enter her work after her ascetic writing experience. We will show that while Duras does destroy meaning, plot and characters in her films, the process of destruction also allows her to foreground the materiality and multisensoriality of cinema.

Her contribution to *Hiroshima mon amour* marked a turning point in her career and had a profound impact on her own filmmaking. Although Duras is known as the scriptwriter of the film, she was also actively involved in its making, and the film was her first practical involvement with cinema. It was followed by the writing of the script of *Une aussi longue absence* (1961), a Franco-Italian film, directed by Henri Colpi. Six years later she co-directed her first film *La Musica* (1966) with Paul Seban.

She made her first film as sole director in 1969 with *Détruire dit-elle*, which set the tone for her future films. Representative of the 1968 period of contestation in France, it is considered to be an example of counter-cinema as it includes a critique of the patriarchal confinement of women (Günther 2002: 17). *Nathalie Granger* (1972) would continue her questioning of patriarchal power structures and the resulting oppression of women. Although resolutely feminist, Duras considered *Nathalie Granger* to be too didactic and, from 1974, with *La Femme du Gange*, she began to experiment with the film form by separating sound and image to further express her contestation of conventions.

Duras' films were often associated with the New Wave, but Renate Günther and Susan Hayward both agree that her films should be considered part of the 1970 avant-garde rather than the New Wave, with its fraternity of male directors which Susan Hayward called the *entre-hommes* (Hayward 1993: 232). Duras' films are much better understood if placed in the context of the 1968 movement, as one of the objectives of her cinema was the dismantling of patriarchal power structures as expressed in society and in mainstream cinema, and the expression of a female-centred perspective. According to Willis:

> Duras' texts exemplify a resistance to consumption and disposability. They demand perpetual rereading; they do not consolidate a singular message that, once received, is finished off in the act of consumption. Rather, they offer an apprenticeship in another form of reading, based on repetition and intertextual circulation. (Willis 1987: 3)

Duras exploited to a great extent the process of recycling and rereading in her films. For example, *Son nom de Venise dans Calcutta désert* reuses the entire soundtrack of *India Song*. Similarly, *L'Homme atlantique*, uses the discarded shots of *Agatha* to create the visual track and 'Aurélia Steiner' is the title of five texts and films. This process of recycling allows the filmmaker a way of reworking her films to free them from what Duras perceived as restrictive film conventions of representation and commerciality. The process of rewriting and constant revising of themes, characters, narratives and of the very materiality of films allows her a deeper investigation and exploration of the medium.

While we have mentioned the many reasons that led Duras to filmmaking, film theorist Laura U. Marks offers interesting insights into film, likely to bring a new understanding of what has been so far understood as Duras' compulsion to destroy writing through the making of film, and each film by making the following. In *The Skin of the Film*, Marks explores intercultural cinema, that is, a cinema at the intersection of two or more cultural regimes of knowledge. She demonstrates the need of intercultural filmmakers to deconstruct film conventions in order to tell stories in their own terms, unhindered by an oppressive dominant film discourse. While Marks analyses films that come from 'new cultural formations of Western metropolitan centres, which in turn have resulted from global flows of immigration, exile, and diaspora' (Marks 2000: 1), they bear many similarities with Duras' filmmaking. Duras was not from a diasporic minority, but she left Vietnam, the place of her childhood, as an adult, and like the filmmakers studied by Marks, attempted to represent, through her writing and films, her experience of living between two cultural regimes. Many of her works focus on memories evoked in her films, especially in the Indian cycle, and like the intercultural films analysed by Marks, her memories are evoked through 'an appeal to non-visual knowledge, embodied knowledge, and experiences of the senses' (Marks 2000: 1) This will be the focus of our study. Marks writes that 'all of us hold knowledge in our bodies and memory in our senses', and she focuses on the question of how film can represent the 'unrepresentable senses such as smell, taste and touch (Marks 2002: xvi), based on memories of unreachable places. This activation of body memory is also how spectators can access the film's sensoriality, through their own body sensations and memories.

The process of dismantling in Duras' films is also one of excavation and archaeological discovery of past memories located in the senses, once freed from the convention of traditional filmmaking. Marks focuses on the haptic appeal of film or what she calls 'the skin of the film' which we will return to in our chapter on the visuality of Duras' films. Marks shows that it is the haptic quality of films that evokes memories of textures and scents, and that exiled filmmakers, unable to revisit their homeland, can reach the material world of those unreachable places through sensory memories. Cinema as a medium which communicates through the senses and perception would have been a very appealing medium for Duras, for whom memories of childhood never ceased to permeate the work. While it would not be appropriate to classify Duras as an intercultural filmmaker, her cinema bears many similarities with the films studied by Marks, who offers a new angle from which to understand Duras' filmic work and the reasons why she turned to cinema. Through sound and image and its closeness to real-life perception, cinema allows Duras to reach layers of sensorial and perceptual memories. As shown by Marks, 'Cinema, by virtue of its richer and muddier semiotic relationship to the world, is all the more an agent of mimesis and synesthesis than writing is' (Marks 2000: 214). Furthermore, Marks explains that 'experimental filmmakers have been exploring the relationships between perception and embodiment for years, offering a mimetic alternative to the mainstream narrativization of experience' (Marks 2000: 215). While many reasons have been put forward by Duras scholars to explain her coming to cinema, the power of the cinematic medium and the capability of its apparatus to represent embodied memories have not yet been explored.

Duras' feminist engagement

As mentioned earlier, the events of May 1968 triggered a radical change in Duras' writing, and led her to direct her own film, *Détruire dit-elle* (1969). As the title suggests, Duras perceived May 1968 as a period of destruction of the old order. All hierarchies had to be challenged, including the gender power structures. *Détruire dit-elle* is the first film which shows the influence of feminism in Duras' work. A few years later she directed *Nathalie Granger* (1972), which is even more clearly a work of exploration of feminism through cinema.

Nathalie Granger was made at a time of intense political activity and theoretical debates in France, following the 1968 students', workers' and women's movement. In April 1971, *Le Nouvel Observateur* had published the Manifesto of the 343, also known as the Manifesto of the 343 Sluts, a declaration signed by 343 women including Duras, who revealed they had had an abortion, thereby risking prosecution, and possibly life sentence, under the 1920 law which forbade abortion. The French women's movement became a powerful force against the anti-abortion and anti-contraception law of 1920. However, it was divided into many small groups, which had their own theories and ideas about feminism. Inspired by Simone de Beauvoir's *Second Sex*, one of the most radical groups held the view that the categories of masculine and feminine are social constructions manufactured by patriarchy. For them, women's liberation depended on the abolition of these categories and the creation of a gender-neutral world. In opposition to this current of feminist thought, Psy & Po (Psychoanalysis and Politics) argued for a feminism of difference. Psy & Po feminists questioned the notion of a gender-neutral society, as it would be adopting masculine values and behaviours. On the contrary, they thought femininity should be revalued and women should create their own identity in harmony with their experiences as women. The theories of Irigaray, Cixous and Kristeva were the basis on which the feminism of difference was constructed and argued. Irigaray, in particular, argued that men and women should develop different subjectivities and that women needed to create their symbolic order, the feminine, based on the representation of female sexuality.

While Duras did not adopt one trend of feminism, she borrowed from both, and both can be observed in her filmic work. She expressed her own ideas on feminism in her interviews with Xavière Gauthier (*Woman to Woman* (1987)), and in *Les Lieux de Marguerite Duras* (1977). These texts indicate that Duras, although very engaged in a feminist reflection, was never one to simply follow mainstream ideas about feminism. On the contrary, she developed her own personal perspective on the notions of the feminine and sexual differences while considering the role of women in a patriarchal society and the family. *Nathalie Granger* clearly explores both of these questions.

In the five interviews conducted by Xavière Gauthier, we can clearly picture the intellectual and feminist context in which Duras was living, writing and making films. These conversations show the development of feminist positions regarding the debates on difference and are part of the reflection of intellectual women on *écriture féminine* (Cixous 1991), on a new female language (Irigaray 1985b) and on the maternal body (Kristeva 1974). Duras explains her perspective on her writing which she links to the unconscious:

> I know that the place where this writes itself, where I write it – when I do – is a place where breathing is shortened and there's a drop on sensory perception. Not everything is heard, only certain things, you see. This is a black and white place. (Duras and Gauthier 1987: 2)

> [T]hese books are painful, to write and to read, and the pain should lead us toward a place… a place of experimentation. What I mean is that they're painful, painful because they're works that move toward an area that's not hollowed out yet, maybe […] This is the blank in the chain you were talking about. I don't mean in psycho-analytic terms … I mean something about what is feminine, you know? (Duras and Gauthier 1987b: 6)

Duras believed writing is located in the unconscious, that women write differently from men, and that to be writers, women have to write from the place of their female desire, not by imitating men's writing. The influence of psychoanalysis is very present in the Gauthier interviews which led Jacques Lacan to publish a famous article 'Hommage à Marguerite Duras' in which he declares: '*Duras* has proved that *she knows* my teachings without being taught by me' (Lacan 2001: 193).

In a 1973 interview with Suzanne Horer and Jeanne Socquet, (Duras 2014c: 169–70), Duras' position on motherhood comes very close to that of Kristeva: a biological experience, a symbiosis between mother and child, that can never be matched by men. According to Duras, the unconditional love between mother and child is *la richesse de la femme* (the wealth of women) (Duras 2014c: 171) and women should not accept to be excluded from it. If this was the case, they would be like men, which she passionately refuses. Women would be cut off from their organic body, the *nuit organique* (organic night) (Duras 2014c: 172). The choice of words is particularly interesting, since Duras used the term *nuit organique* in the context of writing, the organic night being where writing originates. In an interview with Susan Husserl-Kapit in 1973 (Duras 2014c: 172–3), she develops her concept of *écriture féminine*, which rejects men's conception of women's writing as an imitation of the masculine model. She clearly states that feminine writing is a violent and direct form of writing not dictated by the intellect, but on the contrary emanating from a place of silence and darkness, where nothing is thought out beforehand (Duras 2014c: 173). Duras' reflection on French feminism of difference and on *écriture féminine* coincides with her entering a new creative period, a period of exploration of a new medium, cinema, whose materiality is sound and image and no longer the blank page and ink.

In 1976, Michèle Porte conducted interviews with Duras for the national television channel TV1 which led to the publication of *Les Lieux de Marguerite Duras* (reproduced in Duras 2014c). The interview focuses on places where Duras filmed *Nathalie Granger* (1972), *La Femme du Gange* (1974) and *India Song* (1975), and discusses the places and spaces of her childhood in Indochina. In the conversations, Duras strengthens her feminist stance outlined to Gauthier in *Woman to Woman*. She explains that only women can fully inhabit a house: men use the space, but women identify with it, because they are themselves a protective envelope for their baby as a house is for its inhabitants. She also expresses the idea that historically, for women, the house was a place of confinement and a place of work. The themes of *Les Lieux de Marguerite Duras* can clearly be situated within the intellectual context of feminism of difference, which influenced not only Duras' comments on her films but the films themselves. She believes that her creativity springs from what she perceives as a feminine place: an unconscious place, unknown, mysterious; a dark, organic place, away from conventions and learned skill, a pre-symbolic stage. In order to access the feminine creative space she talks about, she had to subvert film and linguistic conventions, representative of a patriarchal order.

Nathalie Granger and feminism

Nathalie Granger is understood by Günther as a militant film, whereas I think it has all the characteristics of an exploration of the concept of difference that was debated at the time of its making rather than a film that aimed at convincing viewers. It is a poetic wandering in the world of women and men and is a highly personal investigation. As a precursor of the more radical films Duras directed later, it is an important work to analyse as it establishes her feminist thinking. It provides the framework for an understanding of what has been identified by scholars as Duras' filmic stylistic devices such as slow shots, silence and music, which are linked to her notions of the feminine.

The film was shot in her own house and garden in Neauphle-le-Château which were the point of departure for the film:

> We always believe that you need to start with a story to make a film. It isn't the case. *For Nathalie Granger*, my point of departure was the house. Completely. I constantly had the house in my head and then a story came to inhabit it, but you see the house was already a film.[2] (Duras 2014c: 196)

Duras always insisted on the importance of spaces, and her choice to shoot *Nathalie Granger*, a film about women, in a private location reveals her desire to make her film a personal exploration of feminist questions.

Her house becomes for her the historical symbol of the imprisonment of generations of women in the home. Recurrent shots of the walls, windows, doors, bars across windows construct the house as a prison-like space, where women are separated from the outside world to do housework and care for children. For example, after the husband's departure, the gaze of the camera rests on a long take of the two women looking out of the dining room as if imprisoned in the house and isolated from the world. There is a strong sense of entrapment as tracking shots show empty corridors and passages that lead to closed doors.

However, the house is also the place of work for women, and the tasks undertaken by them in the home is the subject of the film, as the camera slowly lingers on their hands cleaning the table or ironing children's clothes. These normally invisible female tasks are given the status of work as we hear the steps of women walking around the house and the clattering of the dishes on the soundtrack. In *Les Lieux de Marguerite Duras*, she explains that the house belongs to women and represents the place of female oppression. 'I see Isabelle Granger as a prisoner of the house, prisoner of herself, of her life . . . of this kind of terrible cycle that goes from love for her children to conjugal duties'[3] (Duras 2014c: 186).

The beginning of the *Nathalie Granger* presents binary oppositions between the inside and the outside of the house, the private domestic sphere inhabited by women and children and the social domain associated with men. If the house is shown to be an oppressive space, it is also paradoxically a female space where solidarity between women is formed, time is taken to look, think and wait in silence. Duras' film also equates the house with woman as recipient, the womb and a nurturing space. She explores the effect of the imprisonment of women in the home, what they do with the silence, inertia, stillness and the passivity they are reduced to. It is from this position that Duras elaborates a positive view of the feminine, as a subversive force. What is perceived as oppressive, for example the silencing of women, becomes subversive, a form of resistance when they refuse to speak. Duras seems to provide an answer to the question raised by Irigaray about how silence may be translated into the visual arts and how it relates to female subjectivity. As Irigaray has argued, silence is not only the mark of women's oppression; it can be reclaimed as a form of female resistance and be expressed in their art:

> Is it not safeguarding silence, including in her discourse, that woman can reach a language appropriate to her subjectivity, both external and internal? Is not silence a key of a secular mystery attributed to woman? And does there not now exist a risk of spending or destroying this mystery by willing either to be equal to man or to reverse on the outside our own internal world? Certainly, I am not speaking here of a silence imposed on women but of an economy of silence consciously founded by woman herself. How would it be possible, according to you, to express such a silence in painting? (Irigaray 2004a: 103)

Women's silence is explored in the sequence of *Nathalie Granger* where the salesman (Gérard Depardieu) enters the house to sell a washing machine and finds himself face-to-face with two stubbornly silent women. He confidently utters his well-prepared speech to try to sell them the washing machine, but they look at him, quietly and silently. He continues his speech. One of them interrupts: 'You are not a salesman.' Little by little the salesman loses his confidence and squeezes his attaché case against his stomach, with increasing discomfort. The camera moves from the women to the man, shot reverse shot, in silence. The salesman leaves the room to check what washing machine they own and comes back disheartened; they own the exact machine he has been trying to sell them. The power relation is now reversed. The silence, symptom of the dominated status of the women, becomes their passive strength.

From then on, spectators can perceive silence from a different perspective as women have appropriated it. Silence and pauses reflect the inner space of oppression and the starting point for female interiority and subversion. Irigaray, for whom silence is an opportunity for women to experience the world, themselves, and the other without dissipation, suggests that, as a strategy, a woman should

> insist also and deliberately upon those *blanks* in discourse which recall the places of her exclusion and which, by their *silence plasticity*, ensure the cohesion, the articulation, the coherent expansion of established forms. Reinscribe them hither and thither as *divergencies*, otherwise and elsewhere than they are expected in *ellipses and eclipses* that deconstruct the logical grid of the reader-writer. (Irigaray 1985a: 142)

In our analyses of the sound track, we will return to the use of silence as a sensorial device, independent of the narrative, to be reappropriated by spectators as a lived experience of oppression, exclusion, subversion and the inner world of women.

Context of production, direction and reception

As explained by Bainbridge (2008: 61), any discussion of films directed by women cannot be limited to the textual content of the work. It is important to consider how elements of the films were produced and distributed. The filmic text depends upon extensive processes of production, including approaches to direction and reception that depend on structures of distribution.

Duras needed to film in places she knew well, such as her own house at Neauphle-le-Château in *Nathalie Granger*, in l'hôtel des Roches in Trouville, where she had an apartment, for the films *Agatha et les lectures illimitées* and *L'Homme atlantique*. She also often surrounded herself with people she knew well: technicians, photographers, her own son photographer Jean Mascolo, her musician Carlos d'Alessio, her cameraman Bruno Nuytten, and her preferred actors: Bulle Ogier, Jeanne Moreau, Delphine Seyrig, Gérard Depardieu and Yann Andrea, who was also her lover. It is as if Duras needed to recreate her own familiar environment to make films, which, as we will show, also refract her own sensorial connection to the world. This challenges the definition of autobiography: it is not the retelling and reconstruction of one's life but a conglomeration of elements taken from her life. Duras' films are not autobiographical in a conventional sense but are impregnated by places and people of her life, and those familiar devices were essential to her creativity.

She often shot her films outside with natural light, or in cheap locations, such as her own house as mentioned earlier, the tennis courts of Neauphle-le-Château or Rothschild's dilapidated palace in the Bois de Boulogne. *India Song*, a film about life in India, was shot in or near Paris, but she never thought it necessary to shoot on location. *India Song*, Duras' best-known and most successful film cost a mere 254,542 francs to produce, of which 250,000 came from the National Centre for Cinema (CNC), an agency of the French Ministry of Culture.

In addition, she reused the soundtrack of *India Song* to make *Son nom de Venise dans Calcutta désert*, and the unused shots of *Agatha* to make *L'Homme atlantique*. Duras enjoyed the simplicity of the process of making her films, the recycling of her film material and the desire not to waste, in keeping with her mother's attitude towards money, as she mentioned in several interviews. She never said that she was forced to make films the way she made them: she chose to avoid making expensive, commercial films. She clearly opted for a certain style of film – anti-commercial, anti-establishment, anti-Hollywood – because of her convictions that films had to be intimate, talk about the interiority of characters and subvert the conventions of filmmaking, signs of patriarchal oppression. This mode of production gave her a great deal of freedom. So did the fact that she never attended a film school or learned to direct a film. To her, knowing nothing about filmmaking gave her the freedom to make the films she wanted to make.

Making films on very low budgets, surrounded by a familiar crew, allowed her to work beyond the industrial context, to control the mode of production of her films and to preserve what she considered to be the most important element of her work: her freedom to innovate, to turn her films into works of art and to articulate her female subjectivity in her work. She was free to be a woman who made films without compromise.

Performing authorship and authorial self-inscription

Although filmmaking is by nature collaborative, and, as noted by Bolton, 'the field of authorship studies and the concept of the auteur are contested areas where opinions and positions seem sharply divided' (Bolton 2011: 179), Duras' film authorship is seldom questioned by scholars because she was first known as a novelist and a playwright before becoming a filmmaker, and in her interviews she talked at length about the writing and filming process and of herself as an author. Most of her films were adapted from her own novels and texts or were transformed into written texts after the films were made. In addition, her need to control her work was very strong and has largely contributed to her authorship and her cinematic style which is renowned and easily recognisable. Her collaborators – actors, cameramen, sound engineers, musicians and editors – were also authors in their own rights. When working for Duras they participated in her creative process and put their skills towards her cinematic vision. For all these reasons, scholars have never questioned the notion of film authorship when writing about Duras as a filmmaker.

Martin believes that in order to recognise the contribution of women to films we should move away from the concept of authorship. She advocates replacing film authorship by Agnès Varda's notion of cinécriture:

> A well-written film is also well-filmed, the actors are well-chosen, so are the locations. The cutting, the movement, the points of view, the rhythm of filming and editing have been felt and considered in the way a writer chooses the depth and meaning of sentences, the type of words, number of adverbs, paragraphs, asides, chapters which advance the story or break its flow, etc. In writing it's called style. In the cinema, style is *cinécriture*. (Varda cited by Martin 2008: 132)

For Martin, Varda's concept of cinécriture enables a discussion that acknowledges that the practice of filmmaking *may* not emerge from a single person, but that it is a practice which is organised around a director

(Martin 2008: 132). In her interviews Duras talks about film authorship in traditional terms like Truffaut's or Astruc's ideas of auteurship. However, a close examination of the ways Duras has inscribed herself in her films shows that although she does accept the notion of film auteurship and has little doubt about the fact that she is the auteur of her films, she challenges the traditional representation of the author.

Duras began to insert her presence and her personal world into films with *Nathalie Granger* (1972) by filming her own house in Neauphle-le-Château. She continued this process by using her own voice as a voice-over in *India Song* (1975) and *Son nom de Venise dans Calcultta désert* (1976), by taking the role of the character of the old woman in *Le Camion* (1977), and again providing the voice-over in *Césarée* (1979), *Le Navire Night* (1978), both *Aurélia Steiner* films (1979), *Les Mains négatives* (1979), *Agatha et les lectures illimitées* (1981), and *L'Homme atlantique* (1981). She also filmed her Trouville apartment at length in *Agatha et les lectures illimitées* and gave her partner, Yann Andréa, the main acting role in three of her films.

While Duras' films are not autobiographical depictions, her presence as a disembodied voice and as a character, and the role played by her partner and her own homes can be considered to be contributing to her reflection on the issue of the 'presence' of the author in cinema. Duras never ceased to assert the complexity of her authorial presence in the media and in her films, and reclaimed the filmmaker's voice in a way similar to that of the first person narrator in a novel. The film author, often seen as a conceptual abstraction, at best gender neutral but most of the time assumed to be an authoritative masculine voice, is challenged and re-embodied in Duras' films as a non-authoritarian female voice, or a female body (that of Duras in *Le Camion*).

Subverting further the notion of author in cinema, Duras filmed the mirror reflection of camera and spotlights in several films – *Le Camion, Agatha* and *L'Homme atlantique* – thus acknowledging the film apparatus, which is after all a kind of storyteller or narrator in cinema. She also filmed her own handwritten text (in *Aurélia Steiner*) as further inscription of her presence as author and writer of the film.

Duras' problematisation of the notion of film authorship in cinema has the effect of questioning the concept of subjectivity in cinema, and more precisely that of the female speaking subject. What is the identity of the female speaking subject when she is a disembodied voice and a personal network of relations with actors and spaces? While most spectators would be able to recognise Duras' voice and body, her presence in the film is fragmented, incoherent (does not entirely coincide with a character) and intermedial (as a voice, an image of her body or a written page). Multifaceted, the inscription of the female author reveals a fragmented female subjectivity rather than a coherent, homogenous, unified subject. The presence of familiar spaces, actors and contributors in the films creates a sense of intimacy while not revealing autobiographical details in a traditional way.

Authorship, devoid of its usual representational coherence, is reconceptualised in the films as multiple, and in this way, it is close to Luce Irigaray's theories of the feminine as fluid, fragmented and multiple. But this inscription of the author in the film also foregrounds the materiality of the filmic author, once 'he' has been stripped of his coherent, authoritative and signifying function. The materiality of the author is perceived in the body and the voice, creating the sensation in the spectators that they recognise something of the author at a material and physical level. What is perceived by spectators as the person of the author 'Duras' is the grain of the voice, the intonation, the rhythm of the delivery, the shape, size and gestures of her body or her clothing, and her handwriting, in addition to her style or *cinécriture*. They are all pre-discursive elements. The author becomes part of the audio-visual experience lived by spectators, and part of the aesthetic experience.

The films are a clear product of Duras as the author, but contrary to what appears at first in her interviews, Duras' concept of authorship is in practice not Astruc's notion of *la caméra stylo* or Truffaut's auteur. Rather, Duras expands the notion of authorship, and, as Bolton suggests about female authorship, 'it becomes possible to conceive authorship as process less concerned with *la caméra stylo* than with "a camera speculum"' (Bolton 2011: 195), that acknowledges a constant relationship between filmmaker, character and spectator, enabling the reflection of the interiority of the subject rather than simply the creative work of art of a director (Bolton 2011: 195). Unlike the films examined by Bolton, Duras' films express the subjectivity and interiority of the female author/filmmaker, not solely through the female characters and the narratives, but through the subversion of the medium, and the innovation of the visual and the soundtracks, which can be associated with what Varda has called the style of the filmmaker or *cinécriture*, which I will analyse in the following chapters.

Notes

1 (My translation) 'Ce n'est plus la peine de nous faire le cinéma de l'espoir socialiste. De l'espoir capitaliste. Plus la peine de nous faire celui d'une justice à venir, sociale, fiscale, ou autre.'

2 (My translation) 'On croit toujours qu'il faut partir d'une histoire pour faire du cinema. Ce n'est pas vrai. Pour *Nathalie Granger*, je suis complètement partie de la maison. Vraiment, tout à fait. J'avais la maison en tête constamment, et puis ensuite une histoire est venue s'y loger, voyez, mais la maison, c'était déjà du cinéma.'

3 (My translation) 'Je vois Isabelle Granger comme prisonnière de cette demeure-ci, prisonnière d'elle-même, de sa vie, . . . de cette espèce de circuit infernal qui va de l'amour de ses enfants à ses devoirs conjugaux.'

3

Desynchronisation, subversion and the senses

Over the past ten years, we have discarded one type of theory, gradually switching to another, as yet to be defined, paradigm. Rather than continue to think about the cinema as an ocular-specular phenomenon, whose indexical realism we either celebrated or whose illusionism we excoriated, scholars now tend to regard the cinema as an immersive perceptual event. Body and soundspace, somatic, kinetic and affective sensations have become its default values, and not the eye, the look and ocular verification. (Elsaesser 2003: 120)

However much the spectator may be engaged by plot or genre, subject matter or thematic implication, the texture of the film experience depends centrally upon the moving images and the sound that accompanies them. The audience gains access to story or theme only through that tissue of the sensory materials ... However unaware spectators may be of it, style is working at every moment to shape their experience. (Bordwell 1997: 7–8)

This chapter focuses on one of Duras' most subversive film innovations: the disjunction of sound and image, which is considered to be her idiosyncratic stylistic device. I have shown in a previous study of her cinema (Royer 1997) that such a technique destroys the reality effect created by synchronisation as it indicates to viewers that cinema is not a simple reflection of the world but a complex and artificial medium. In this chapter, I would like to examine the effect of such a device on spectators' sensorial perceptions as they relate to Duras' obsession with memories, the most important theme of her films.

It took Duras several years of experimenting with filmmaking before she began using the technique of desynchronisation of sound and image. The power of the voice and of speech was always a central preoccupation in her writing and filmmaking, and the female voice-over has an important role in her first film collaboration *Hiroshima mon amour* (1959). Later, in her first solo films, *Détruire dit-elle* (1969) and *Nathalie Granger* (1972), voices and images are synchronised, but neither of the films has a linear narrative or is plot-driven. In addition, both films have fragmented, elliptic dialogues, punctuated by long silences, and there is an extensive use of voices off-screen. So the transgression of audio-visual conventions started with Duras' very first experimentations with filmmaking, but it is only with her third film *La Femme du Gange* (1974) that Duras took the step to clearly split the visual track and the soundtrack. Her journey in the art of filmmaking towards the destruction of synchronisation was progressive and shows that she was aware of the importance of such a transgression and the risk it represented. This chapter will look first at what the disjunction of sound and image brings to Duras' filmmaking that synchronisation was unable to achieve, before examining the effects on spectators of this innovative technique.

In the early days of cinema, sound was limited to music played by a musician in the movie theatre, and its function was to cover the noise of the projector. Later, sound was integrated into the film itself and its role became more and more sophisticated: in addition to creating the atmosphere of the film, it aimed at emphasising the emotions already triggered by the images on-screen. The soundtrack supplemented the visual track and became totally dependent on the plot and the images. Synchronisation quickly became the rule. Although synchronisation appears very natural to film spectators, it is an artificial device that contributes to realism and to creating the impression of unity of film characters, and reinforces the spatial and temporal coherence of the plot.

Synchronisation, however, as pointed out by leading French scholar Michel Chion, leads to the obliteration of the sound: 'Synchronous sounds as such are most often forgotten, swallowed by the plot, and . . . their meaning, their effects are thought to be generated by the image or by the film in its globality'[1] (Chion 1985: 14). Such a realistic device can seem tyrannical and limiting for filmmakers who want to create a polysemic and polyphonic film and it is therefore not entirely surprising if Duras, an innovative writer who became a filmmaker, rebelled against such a subjugation of sound, and particularly the voice, to the image. The subversion of film conventions and renewal of film poetics reflected her profound desire to innovate in her creative work. They can also be explained by the intellectual atmosphere of the 1970s anti-establishment and French feminist movements of the period.

As mentioned in previous chapters, Duras' involvement with the 1968 movement and with feminism is reflected in several films at the narrative level, for example in *Détruire dit-elle* and *Nathalie Granger*. However, Duras expressed her feminist ideas not only through a disconnected and fragmented narrative but also, as explained by Günther, by introducing a counter-cinematic model of female subjectivity with 'a female film language . . . reflected in her cinematographic technique' (Günther 2002: 96). For Duras, conventional films reproduce the power structures of society, and by deconstructing cinematic strategies of representation such as actors' embodiment, synchronisation, the use of music and silence, she is subverting the established film hierarchies and power structures at work within the conventions of filmmaking. The desynchronisation of sound and image was for Duras one of the devices that could destabilise these hierarchies.

In his book *Essais sémiotiques,* Christian Metz points to the confusion that exists about the notion of sound 'off' showing that a sound is thought to be 'off' when it is in fact the origin of the sound that is not shown on-screen. A 'voice-over' is actually the voice of a character that does not appear on-screen. Metz notes that a sound itself is in fact never 'off' and that this expression reveals the hierarchy between sound and image in cinema. One claims to be speaking about sound when in fact they are thinking about the visual source of the sound (Metz 1977: 157–8). In Duras' desynchronised films, since all the sounds are 'off-screen', their source becomes irrelevant. Detached from the image, sounds can be heard independently of the visual track and the plot. They can be appreciated for their aural qualities, and when they come into contact with the image, spectators can weave meanings and let their imaginations work freely. This produces a poetic effect which will now be examined. This will be followed by an exploration of how desynchronisation affects spectators' reception and perception.

Desynchronisation, poetic effect, memory and embodiment

In several of Duras' films, there is no correlation between sound and image, as is the case with *Aurélia Steiner (Melbourne)*: a voice (that of Duras) reads a love letter to an unknown recipient, recalling 2,000 years of violence and suffering while on the screen slow travelling shots (the camera is on a barge) show the lights on the banks of the river Seine and their shimmering reflections on the water, punctuated by very dark shots when the camera goes under bridges. The peaceful, beautiful images contrast with the soundtrack, heightening the effects of the images and their materiality: framing, light, colours, movement, the sense of liquidity and of flowing movement are foregrounded. They also exacerbate the impact of the narrative voice as it recounts stories of extreme violence, triggering the imagination of listeners in a way similar to the reading process, as in the following example:

> Killing has happened here.
> Did you know about it?
> Killing, yes.
> Almost every day. For a thousand years. Thousands and thousands of years.
> Yes. Once. A thousand times. One hundred thousand.
> Bloodied river.[2]

At times, sound and the visual can be linked almost by accident, words and images weave subtle connections and analogies, and metaphoric associations can be formed by spectators.

The poetic effect can also suddenly emerge from a paradoxical encounter of voice and image. Such is the case when the voice describes the 'blue and empty liquid of your eyes' as a barge carrying black coal passes by. Dominique Noguez (1984: 58) points out the pleasure derived by spectators from these contradictory evocations of conflicting colours and textures, *une rencontre miraculeuse* (a miraculous encounter) that surprises and disturbs. These contrasts are a very common occurrence in the films of Duras who was very fond of oxymoron, a poetic device that the disjunction of sound and image can easily create. Central to Duras' filmic style, its effects on spectators is best understood by examining *Agatha et les lectures illimitées* (1981) which is entirely constructed around an oxymoronic structure.

In *Agatha et les lectures illimitées* the visual track shows a wintery sea landscape in cold bluish colours, while the voices remember the story of an incestuous love between a brother and a sister in the heat of the summer months. The separation of sound and image reproduces stylistically the process of the remembering of past events narrated by the voice. It superimposes two spatial and temporal events: a deserted hotel in Trouville in winter on the visual track and seaside holidays in summer on the soundtrack, provoking in spectators the very experience of memory when two different times and locations collide. The effect of such a situation on the sensorial experience of viewers is complex and will now be examined by focusing on the perception of temperature by spectators or thermoception.

In his book *The Multisensory Film Experience: a Cognitive Model of Experiential Film Aesthetics*, Antunes shows that our brain can perceive an audio-visual medium in a multisensory manner because it is our natural way of perceiving and a process which is not within our control. He also points out that 'spectators can perceive temperature through an audio-visual medium such as films, where there is no contact with the thermal energy of the film's world' (Antunes 2016: loc. 3023). It is through sight and hearing that spectators are able to access these perceptual experiences. Hence, the perception of temperature or thermoception combines several elements: it is associative, intellectual and imaginative, but viewers are often unaware of the way the sensation of temperature is triggered.

With *Agatha et les lectures illimitées*, Duras experiments with the possibility of cinema to reproduce her own embodied experience of memory and her hybrid self with two different sensorial environments being lived simultaneously: her memories are not solely represented by the narration of a story but by the reconstitution of perceptual experiences facilitated by the dissociation of the visual and the auditory. In *Agatha et les lectures illimitées*, if we follow Antunes' theories on thermoception, spectators would experience cold and heat simultaneously through the disjunction of sound and image and their multisensory qualities.

The embodied memory of tropical heat, which may be for Duras a childhood memory, and the experience of the wintery cold can cohabitate through the disjunction of sound and image. Although – apart from the Indian cycle which refers directly to an Asian experience – Duras' films do not explicitly represent a multicultural environment, they express the experience of living between cultures, not through a realistic plot, but by the way the filmic conventions are disrupted and the split between image and sound allows for two different perceptual worlds to come into contact.

Most films written and directed by Duras which stage the process of remembering – *Hiroshima mon amour* (1959); films of the Indian cycle; short films *(Aurélia Steiner* series (1979); *Les Mains négatives* (1978); *Césarée* (1978)); *L'Homme atlantique* (1981) and *Il Dialoguo di Roma* (1982) – use the voice-over and desynchronisation to provide viewers with the embodied experience of memory while telling a story of remembering. This shows Duras' obsession with the past and a desire to understand and explore the role of the sensorial body in the process of remembrance, through film.

According to Marks, 'a number of intercultural works engage sense memories, and memories of touch in particular, by exploiting the relative weakness of the visual image – the lack of things to see' (Marks 2000: 153). In *Agatha et les lectures illimitées*, not only is the sense of touch explored, as we will see in the chapter on visuality, but thermoception is experienced through 'the lack of things to see' as no action takes places on the screen, while a rich soundtrack engages sense memories. At the same time, the aesthetic experience is heightened by the disjunction of the two tracks, which renders an intellectual approach to the film useless at the time of viewing since it is the unconscious perception of the lived body which is called upon. Desynchronisation perturbs logical thinking and, to use Kennedy's expression, leads to a 'material capture of the experience' (Kennedy 2000: 47) rather than an intellectual one.

Representing the unrepresentability of pain through audio-visual disjunction

In several interviews and articles, Duras expressed the impossibility of showing horrific events such as the destruction of Hiroshima or the image of deportees in concentration camps: 'All we can do is to speak of the impossibility of speaking about Hiroshima,' she writes (Duras 2014b: 8), and in *Hiroshima mon amour* (1959), Resnais and Duras agreed about the unrepresentability of atomic devastation. According to Jennifer Barker in *The Tactile Eye: Touch and the Cinematic Experience* (2009), the film suggests 'that it is only through touch that the lovers can experience the truth of themselves, each other, and the past' (Barker 2009: 57) and not through representation. She also believes that the documentary footage of survivors creates a separation between image and viewers, and while it is 'emotionally moving' it does not touch spectators 'as intimately as one must in order [for them] to understand' (Barker 2009: 58). I would argue that it is not only through touch that the past of Hiroshima can be accessed, but it is also through the complex relation between sound and image and the impossibility of representing it in a coherent and logical manner that spectators are 'touched'. Spectators are able to see confronting images of burnt bodies, deformed limbs and monstrous foetuses kept in jars at the Hiroshima museum, while the soft voice of Emmanuelle Riva comments on the photos of scorched metal, suspended human flesh as if still alive and its agony still fresh, and charred and shattered stones. An anempathetic music accompanies some of the shots, and when the camera lingers on the rooms and corridors of the hospital, a Japanese voice repeats: 'You didn't see the hospital in Hiroshima, you saw nothing in Hiroshima.' While a coherent and linear narrative and the visual track cannot represent the extent of the devastation of Hiroshima and of the suffering that accompanied it, and an empathic reaction is not triggered by character representation, that does not mean spectators are not affected by the images of the film and by the fragmented audio-visual rendering of the experience. On the contrary, *Hiroshima mon amour* elicits in spectators what Antunes has called 'nociceptive experiences':

> Spectators have the capacity to access these experiences in the realm of their actual sensations. Pain is not a sensation that enters our awareness exclusively through skin contact with noxious stimuli; instead, pain can be triggered by higher elements of our cognition. Moreover, it is a sensory modality that is informed not exclusively by the nociceptors in our skin tissues, joints and muscles, but also by visual and auditory information in a manner that makes it (in line with other senses) a multisensory modality. (Antunes 2016: loc. 2246–52)

In *Hiroshima mon amour*, spectators are affected by the images they perceive independently of the narrative, and the contrast between the two tracks compounds the effects. Because of the fragmented narrative and the use of the non-diegetic voice-over, the narrative does not drive the emotions felt by spectators. It is the materiality of the image (close-ups of wounds and burnt skulls, for example) and the sound (the soft voice of Emmanuelle Riva retelling her own story and the story of Hiroshima in a fragmented narrative) that triggers nociception, not the process of representation. In *Hiroshima mon amour*, there is an aesthetics of pain that will become an important characteristic of Duras' filmic style and is located in the audio-visual poetics of the films.

A similar but perhaps more extreme situation is happening in *Aurélia Steiner (Vancouver)*, where a voice (that of Duras) tells the story of the birth of a baby girl in a death camp during World War II, while a still shot shows rows of silver birches with their tall naked trunks. There is no visual human representation of the deported waiting in the desolated landscape, and no identification process with the characters, but metaphoric shots filmed from the point of view of what could be the mother watching prisoners in the camp, and which can loosely be connected to the soundtrack. Duras' voice explains:

> My mother died in childbirth under the wooden benches of the camp. Dead, burnt with the contingent of deportees sent to the gas chamber. Aurelia Steiner my mother looks at the white rectangle of the camp courtyard in front of her. Her agony is long. Beside her, the child is alive.[3] (Duras 2014c: 504)

This is followed by a long silence.

While there is no visual representation of the scene narrated by the voices, what is produced by the film is the atmosphere of the event. The black and white images, the wintery cold and the female voice recounting the story combine to trigger in spectators powerful multiple sensory experiences such as feelings of cold, desolation, isolation and sadness. As previously mentioned, the disjunction of the two tracks compounds the effects without annihilating the independent auditory and visual perceptions. The spectators' individual images of the dead mother and the birth of the child, according to their own history and story, the silence and the metaphoric visual shots are opened to individual experiences, similar to the experience of reading a poem. Colours, intonation of the voice, rhythm of the sentences, and the image of the rows of trees provide an aesthetic and sensorial experience of the camps. Thermoception, nociception, ocular and auditory perceptions combine to provide an embodied experience of the event but not its representation. Rather than being distanced, spectators gain access to some kind of mediated suffering through the proximity of the voice and the tissues of sensory materials created by Duras' stylistic devices. As explained by Michel Chion (1999), hearing creates a sense of proximity between listeners and the film whereas the gaze implies distance between the viewer and the object of the gaze. By disconnecting sound and image and shifting the primacy of the film to the auditory at the expense of the ocular, Duras' films create a sense of intimacy with the sensory world of the films.

These strategies are repeated throughout the film. There is no visual representation of Jewish deportees, only a metonymic allusion through an image of deserted train stations, train carriages loaded with tree trunks with tattooed numbers and letters on their flesh-like surface (Figure 3.1).

Figure 3.1 *Aurélia Steiner (Vancouver)* (DVD)

It is only through the imagination and personal experience of spectators, and the shots of the desolated landscape supported by a few clues, that the experience takes place. As in *Hiroshima mon amour*, the dissociation of sound and image allows the expression of the impossibility of representing the concentration camp and the death of the mother, but the multisensory experience of the scene is still elicited by the voice, the poetry of images and repeated silences. Horror and aesthetics merge.

In *Césarée* (1979), love and suffering are also left off-screen: some correlations between sound and image are sometimes suggested. A female voice (that of Duras) evokes the Palestinian city of Césarée and Bérénice, the 'queen of the Jews', repudiated for reasons of state. The voice speaks of the pain of abandonment and destruction while on the screen an extremely slow track shot shows deserted Parisian streets and les jardins des Tuileries. The impossibility of representing passion and pain is reinforced by the unusually quiet images of Paris. The monophonic intonation of the voice off-screen refuses any kind of expressionism. The film, however, manages to trigger embodied feelings of pain and sadness by the lack of visual and aural representation, silence, inexpressive voice-over, Paris emptied of its tourists and inhabitants, combined with the extreme passion narrated by the voice. Spectators can experience the invisibility of passion, the void and a sense of emptiness and sadness that are depicted on the soundtrack.

The feelings of lack and absence are further explored in *Le Navire Night* (1979) in the voices of Benoît Jacquot and Marguerite Duras who read the text of the same name which tells the love story of two people who communicate essentially by telephone. The two lovers never meet, and their desire can be sustained by constantly postponing its satisfaction. The visual track presents us with shots of Paris, a park, le Bois de Boulogne, the Seine and the Père Lachaise cemetery. Several sequences are filmed inside a house where actors Matthieu Carrière, Bulle Ogier and Dominique Sanda are shown, but it is impossible to link the actors to the characters evoked on the soundtrack. Traditionally, as already mentioned, synchronisation gives rise to redundancy, excess in representation as the sound doubles what is represented on the screen. The disruption of the unit sound/image to such an extreme as is the case in *Le Navire Night* leads to spectators physically feeling 'lack' as a lived embodied feeling and not simply as the expression of an absence; it is like the negative of a photograph through which the violence of passion can still be perceived. In this film, desynchronisation leads to challenging the act of looking, which is also at the centre of the story as the two lovers cannot see each other, and to the re-evaluation of the voice and more generally of sound. What can be said in the gaps opened by the audio-visual disjunction moves spectators away from a logical understanding of film and narrative and exposes them to the sensorial world of what is experienced by the two lovers: the pleasure located in the lack of the other's presence and in the sound of his/her voice.

Luce Irigaray has suggested that the emphasis on the visual in patriarchal societies has contributed to the exclusion or the invisibility of female subjectivities which may be constructed through other senses than the visual, such as touch and the auditory. The disjunction of sound and image resonates with Irigaray's strategies to undo the expression of masculine subjectivities in film and to begin to put into place female subjectivities that lead to an emphasis on sensoriality and aurality. Was this a conscious process for Duras, who was exposed to the feminist ideas of her time as shown in previous chapters? It is impossible to answer that question with certainty, but what can be said is that she recognised herself in these strategies as shown in her interviews, and undoubtedly consciously experimented with them in her films.

Actors, movements and vestibular perception

Because of the disjunction between sound and image, actors do not embody specific characters, they symbolise or tell an experience through their movements and their use of space. The film creates a void, a distance between actors and characters. Renate Günther suggests that spectators can then project their own version of the character, for example their own representation of Anne-Marie Stretter in *India Song*. I would add that this also brings up the material reality of a film character: a voice and the image of a body that moves through space. Colours of the clothes, the body of the actor, her hair, her skin, the slow wandering of actors through space are the elements that are foregrounded.

One of the remarkable aspects of Duras' films is the way actors move in the film. Their pace is slow, their movements are as if in slow motion, regardless of what the voices narrate. Antunes has examined the spectators' sense of movement in films and suggests that the vestibular is an important aspect of their perception: 'Although we are in a seated position, the vestibular shapes our perceptual experience of a film at all times. Much of the perceptual information that we commonly believe to be purely visual is actually also vestibular' (Antunes 2016: loc. 1161). What Antunes refers to with the term 'vestibular' is our sense of orientation and balance which is also related to proprioception, the unconscious perception of movement and spatial orientation. In our chapter on the visual track we will examine the effect of the mirror shots so common in Duras' films on proprioception and the vestibular sense. In the present chapter, on the split between sound and image, the question of the effect of slow motion of actors on the screen combined with disconnected sound is interesting to raise. Many of viewers' embodied responses to film are not under their control, and according to Antunes, they can combine several senses simultaneously:

> The multisensory nature of human perception shows not only that it is possible for spectators to have vestibular experiences when viewing a film, but also that it would be impossible to completely isolate visual and auditory experiences from vestibular information. (Antunes 2016: loc. 1306)

Neuroscience, especially the discovery of mirror neurons, is having an increasing impact on the way we understand cinema and is especially useful to an understanding of what is happening to spectators when watching actors on the screen. Mirror neurons are considered to aid imitation and be the basic building blocks of our understanding and knowledge formation. They allow viewers to sense what is happening in front of them, not only in life but also on-screen. According to Elliott:

> Mirror neurons suggest that we understand those around us not through identification, empathy and sympathy but through neurological processes that evoke the movements of others within ourselves – that when we see someone eating, the same neurons are fired in our brains as if we ourselves were eating. (Elliott 2010: 11)

This is happening at a bio-neurological level and is mostly unconscious. It allows spectators to feel what characters express on-screen without reasoning, as their bodies and brains simulate what is presented to them. Elliott suggests that

> what is interesting and vital to an understanding of how mirror neurons can inform film theory is that, in humans, movies do produce results. In a study by Fogassi et al., films of hand actions were witnessed by a series of subjects and the resulting mirror neurons were activated; suggesting that for humans, at least, cinema is as real as life. (Elliot 2010: 11)

This process has been called by Vittorio Gallese 'embodied simulation', a mechanism by which our brain/body system models its interaction with the world (Gallese and Guerra 2012b). Duras' films are often described as hypnotic, provoking a sense of rapture and disorientation, and the notion of embodied simulation can help us understand the effect of her films on spectators. Actors move very slowly, silently, they often stand motionless, and as the disjunction of image and sound provides no compensation for the lack of action, spectators are left to experience the lethargy in their own body through the process of embodied simulation.

Nathalie Granger provides an interesting clue as to how to understand the character's extreme passivity as the film is a feminist statement on women's oppression in the domestic sphere. Women in *Nathalie Granger* are bored, often silent. As seen in our previous chapter, their life seems meaningless, without the possibility to exercise any initiative, imprisoned in their home and body. In none of Duras' films are female characters active: they move slowly as if oppressed or imprisoned by external forces, a bodily expression of female oppression similar to that of the characters of *Nathalie Granger*.

In several films, there is no visual representation of characters at all, no actors on-screen; there are only voices on the soundtrack, narrative voices or voices of characters. This is the case of *Son nom de Venise dans Calcutta désert*, *Aurélia Steiner (Melbourne)*, *Aurélia Steiner (Vancouver)*, *Les Mains négatives* and *Césarée*. In other films, actors are used perhaps to stand as characters, but it is not always their voices that are heard. Duras' voice, for instance, reads the dialogues of the sister and the brother in *Agatha et les lectures illimitées*, but she does not appear on-screen; Bulle

Ogier and Yann Andrea function as the characters' visual appearances. The disruption of filmic characters has for effect the questioning of the representation of subjectivities through character representation. If we are to analyse female subjectivity in the films of Duras, it is not through female characters that it can be achieved. The fragmentation of female protagonists, the extreme passivity and slowness of actors standing in for them, and their aural, rather than visual, presence can be associated with Irigaray's theories on the feminine, and it is through the whole process of a different type of filmmaking rather than through character representation that female subjectivity can be analysed.

Duras is not the only female filmmaker to have made an original use of sound and synchronisation. 'Campion, Coppola and Ramsay all use sound, and its relationship with the image and narrative, to create original 'soundscapes' ... as expressive of subjectivity and interiority' (Bolton 2011: 177). Like Duras, they work within and outside the visual. However, Duras' films were produced in the context of feminism of difference and she was aware of the political implications of her film innovations, as shown in the interviews she gave about her films, for example with Xavière Gauthier in *Woman to Woman*, mentioned in the previous chapter. While the characters of *Détruire dit-elle* and *Nathalie Granger* provide a clear message on female subjectivities, their lethargy and lack of action being signs of their oppression, in desynchronised films it is the entire film that instils the bodily effect of female oppression. In order to provoke these embodied feelings in spectators, Duras had to disturb filmic conventions, especially the relationship between sound and image. Spectators are put in a situation where they experience feelings of lack, lethargy, oppression and pain through the film devices, not through character identification.

Desynchronisation and synaesthesia

In their article on synaesthesia, Laine and Strauven discuss the use of the notion of synaesthesia in the humanities in the last decade. They note that synaesthesia 'became the new catchword in various fields of scientific research and artistic practice. The concept made its noteworthy entrance from psychology and neuroscience into the realm of the arts, computer graphics, and (new) media and cinema studies' (Laine and Strauven 2009: 249), and a large number of publications have recently appeared on the subject.

Synaesthesia refers to intersensory relations and the ability of one sense to trigger another, and, according to Cytowic's thesis (2002), we experience synaesthesia below the level of our consciousness. As explained by Elliott, 'the synaesthetic links between vision and the other senses, and vision and memory, impact greatly upon our notion of what constitutes the process of cinema spectatorship' (Elliott 2010: 84). For Elliott, this means that

> when we watch a film for instance, our minds can be having one experience (of the narrative, of character empathy, of political, sexual and ideological interpolation and so on), whereas our bodies and our limbic systems could be having another, altogether a different experience, one that is rooted in our past, in our sensual memory and in synaesthesis, where visual inputs trigger gustatory or tactile sensations. (Elliott 2010: 84)

Film is the result of the intertwining of many elements – camerawork; editing; light, colour and sound design; and our perceptual, multisensory nature as spectators – and, although it consciously engages only two senses, it 'activates a memory that necessarily involves all the senses' (Marks 2000: 40). Beugnet goes even further:

> Through framing, camera movement, light and contrast, the grain of the image and the mix of different film stocks, as well as the variations of sound and visual intensities, the effect of the audio-visual footage extends to touch, smell and taste, and, in turn, operates as a relay between the sensual and the emotional – the diffuse but pervasive multi-sensory evocation of pleasure, desire, longing, fear and terror. (Beugnet 2007: 74)

The desynchronisation process, by undermining the narrative and thematic focus, appeals to all the senses at once. As shown with the examples of thermoception and nociception, intersensory perception is constantly activated in Duras' films. The audio-visual disjunction multiplies the synaesthetic effects as each track provokes its own synaesthetic network of reactions.

Instead of being told what happens and hearing dialogues about the motivations behind the actions of characters and events, her films resort to a level of experiential aesthetics based on the power of images, of sounds and of words to trigger the senses. The disjunction of sound and image offers an increased freedom of the filmic elements to elicit personal memories beyond the limits of representation. The Duras spectator does not experience cinema as an exercise in the mastery of a representational system, but as the triggering of what Sobchack has referred to as a 'pre-logical non-hierarchical unity of the sensorium' (Sobchack 2004: 69). This notion can be linked to Irigaray's and Kristeva's theories on the feminine, with their insistence on the importance of a prelinguistic stage that favours the sense of touch and other senses, as mentioned earlier. In our next chapter we will examine in detail the synaesthetic effects of the visual: how visual perception can extend to the senses of touch and smell.

Notes

1   (My translation) 'Les sons dits synchrones sont le plus souvent oubliés en tant que tels, avalés par la fiction, et . . . leur sens, leur effet est en général mis au compte de l'image seule ou de cet objet global qu'est le film.'

2   (My translation) 'On a tué, ici/vous le saviez?/tué, oui/Presque chaque jour. Pendant mille ans. Mille et mille ans/Oui. Une fois. Mille fois. Cent mille/ le fleuve ensanglanté.'

3   (My translation) 'Ma mère est morte en couches sous les bat-flanc du camp. Brûlée morte avec les contingents des chambres à gaz. Aurélia Steiner ma mère, regarde devant elle le grand rectangle blanc de la cour de rassemblement du camp. Son agonie est longue. A ses côtés l'enfant est vivante.'

4

Multisensorial visuality

Contemporary neuroscience shows that what we see is not the simple 'visual' recording in our brain of what stands in front of our eyes, but the result of a complex construction whose outcome is the result of the fundamental contribution of our body with its motor potentialities, our senses and emotions, our imagination, and our memories. We must definitely abandon the out-dated concept of solipsistic and 'purely visibilist' vision. Vision is a complex experience, intrinsically synesthetic, that is, made of attributes that largely exceed the mere transposition in visual coordinates of what we experience any time we lay our eyes on something. (Gallese 2017b: 20)

Haptic images can give the impression of seeing for the first time; gradually discovering what is in the image rather than coming to the image already knowing what it is. (Beugnet 2008: 178)

Little attention has been given to the visual track by Duras scholars, who have focused on the unconventional narratives of the films, partly because there is a clear tendency towards rarefaction of the image – to the point of including twenty minutes of black screen in *L'Homme atlantique* – and partly because of the unusual richness of the soundtracks and in particular the narrative voice. Duras worked with the best cinematographer and film editors of her time: Bruno Nuytten, Pierre L'Homme, Dominique Le Rigoleur, Ghislain Cloquet, Sacha Verny and Dominique Auvray. This is surely a sign that more attention should be directed towards understanding her use of the filmic image and its effects on spectators. When studying the visual tracks, scholars have focused on the destructive process that progressively saps visuality to its ultimate culmination, the absence of image, but the richness and aesthetics of the visual tracks are as exceptional and innovative as the soundtracks and produce on the reception of the film a strong impact which deserves analysis.

In the recently published series of interviews *Le Livre dit. Entretiens de Duras filmé* (2014c), Duras underlines the importance she gave to the visual aesthetics of her films, to the framing of shots, lighting and colours, especially in *Agatha et les lectures illimitées*, and mentions at length her collaboration with her directors of photography. New theories on haptic visuality and the multisensoriality of the image have led me to rethink Duras' visual tracks and to study them independently of the sound. As we will see, her cinema is not only asking us to listen differently but also to see in other ways.

This is all the more interesting as gender theories have stressed the role of vision in the patriarchal objectification of women. Laura Mulvey's article 'Visual Pleasure and Narrative Cinema' (1975), claims that the male gaze has defined cinematic visuality, firstly, because the camera represents the male gaze and objectifies women's bodies and secondly, because spectators, assumed to be male, enjoy the film from the perspective of a heterosexual man. Irigaray has also stressed the role of vision in the patriarchal objectification of women and has called for a style that 'does not privilege sight; instead it takes each figure back to its source, which is among other things tactile' (Irigaray 1985b: 79). Considering the importance of recent research on the tactility of film and the notion of the haptic, Irigaray's suggestion is very significant. Analysing the visual track will therefore not be limited to examining its impact in the realm of visual perception. On the contrary, taking into consideration the numerous studies undertaken by film scholars on the multisensorial effects of visual perception, I will focus on the multi- and intersensoriality of images, drawing parallels with Irigaray's theories on what I would call a new visuality.

Intercultural memories

Marks, in her book *The Skin of the Film: Intercultural Cinema, Embodiment, and the Senses*, argues that intercultural cinema evokes memories of culture and place, through an appeal to non-representative knowledge, embodied knowledge and experiences of the senses, such as touch, smell and taste (Marks 2000: 2). Duras' own words on how memory is triggered point to a similar process of embodiment of sensorial memories, which can resurface in places and spaces. To Laura Adler, who was suggesting going to Indochina to help her write her biography, she remarked:

> You won't find anything in Vietnam. Get Yann to take you to the banks of the Seine, thirty kilometres outside of Paris, where the river loops, where the leaves make a bed on the banks and where the earth has grown spongy. It isn't *like* the Mekong. It *is* the Mekong. (Adler 2001: 9)

Similarly, Agnès Varda explained in 1961: 'I believe that people are made of the places they love or have lived in; I believe that location inhabits and propels us' (Michaud and Bellour 1961: 14). Duras' visual tracks are filled with shots of landscapes – the sea, the river and the beach – and with empty rooms and at times immobile or slow-moving actors. The slow-tracking shots interrupted by long still shots and the extreme close-ups give the impression that the camera scrutinises the space as if to try to unearth past sensory artefacts from what is gazed at.

Because of the lack of action and coherent plot and the slow rhythm of the films, what Marks calls the materiality of the visual track, such as textures, light and colours, comes to the forefront for spectators. Duras' films offer viewers a different type of looking, as they are not drawn into the action of the film but are asked to gaze at the images as images. The visual track allows spectators to linger, explore the space, search the close-ups, rather than establishing its domination and control over the viewers' gaze. The relationship between director, spectators and the film and its characters is no longer hierarchical but, to use Bolton's expression, horizontal (Bolton 2011: 194).

In her studies on intercultural cinema, Marks provides a careful examination of the senses, such as touch and smell, which cannot be represented directly by cinema but are triggered by the visual tracks. She argues that the way intercultural film signifies is through a contact between perceiver and object rather than through representational narratives. She uses the term haptic vision to refer to the area of vision that allows the appreciation of texture, of surface and movement and hence relates the sense of sight to the rest of the sensorium: 'While optical perception privileges the representative power of the image, haptic perception privileges the material presence ... haptic visuality involves the body more than is the case with optical visuality' (Marks 2000: 162). Hapticity is more synaesthetic than optical vision, because it connects sight to our senses. Haptic images are, however, to be experienced rather than understood. For Deleuze (2003), haptic vision questions the frontiers between what the eyes see and what the hand feels, between object and subject, and provides new ways of linking what we see and how we feel.

In this chapter, I seek to explore the tactility of Duras' films, their texture, space, rhythm and kinaesthetics, and examine how they may affect not so much the viewers' intellects but their sensorial bodies. To quote Barker in *The Tactile Eye: Touch and the Cinematic Experience* (2009), I wish to reveal a new 'sensually formed (and informed) understanding of the ways that meaning and significance emerge in and are articulated through the fleshy, muscular and visceral engagement that occurs between films and viewers' bodies' (Barker 2009: 4).

Hapticity

Touching evokes closeness and intimacy, and while many scholars have examined the representation of desire in Duras' films, paradoxically few have mentioned the sense of touch triggered by the visual images of the films. Although *Hiroshima mon amour* was not directed by Duras, she actively contributed to its making, and many aspects of the film inspired the films she later directed. A brief analysis of *Hiroshima mon amour* will provide a useful start to the study of hapticity in the films she later directed.

In her study, Barker analyses *Hiroshima mon amour* to show that 'history, memory and loss manifest themselves visibly and sensuously in the press of skin against skin, both within the film and between film and viewer' (Barker 2009: 57). The first images in *Hiroshima mon amour* represent two bodies in an embrace, and as we see no faces, it is difficult to differentiate the two bodies which seem to be fused (Figure 4.1). As Martin points out, 'we cannot pinpoint where one skin ends and another begins, since this initial sequence is filmed as a close-up on human skin accompanied only by the musical score

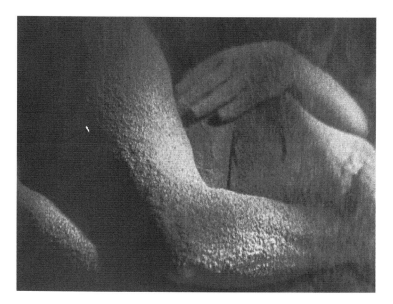

Figure 4.1 *Hiroshima mon amour* (DVD)

by Giovanni Fusco' (Martin 2013: 267). What is emphasised in this sequence is the textured surface, which Duras describes in her text as covered by ash, rain, dew or perspiration (Duras 2011b: 15). The extreme close-up creates a blurring effect because of the grainy quality of the shot combined with a dissolve. Our eyes become less a means to understand the meaning of the image and more like fingers feeling the grain of the skin, its temperature and its humidity. As suggested by Martin, the technique of the dissolve is perfectly suited to the material filmed, one shot dissolving into the other:

> With its careful attention to tactile surfaces and textures, Resnais's initial sequence appeals to what Laura Mulvey has termed a 'haptic visuality' – images that invite the viewer to respond to the image as a tactile experience, to use vision as though it were sense of touch. (Martin 2013: 268)

Barker rightly explains that the film 'invites our pleasure by taking its own pleasure in the form of sensuous dissolves, for example, and invites our horror by being horrified, which it expresses with a startling whip pan' (Barker 2009: 68). Although Barker uses the terms 'understand' and 'make sense of' the shots, spectators are unable to have an intellectual approach to the beginning of the film, it is only a posteriori that they are able to make sense of the opening shots. At the time of viewing, they can only have a perceptual reception of what they see on-screen. It is the viewers' senses that respond to the film, and according to neuroscientists and phenomenologists, it happens unconsciously and 'without a thought' (Sobchack 2004: 65).

In *Hiroshima mon amour*, the sense of touch is often registering pleasure and these initial examples of haptic visuality focus on a scene of desire and are felt by spectators as pleasant. However, several sequences in the film give the viewer a painful sensation, as we explained in our previous chapter, especially when the camera lingers in a close-up on a man's scalp, burnt and scarred, or shows the eyelid of a Hiroshima victim to reveal a gaping hole. Then there are the shots of the exhibits in the Hiroshima museum consisting of pieces of human skin floating in a jar of murky liquid, as Emmanuelle Riva's voice-over talks about the human skins floating, surviving, still in the freshness of their sufferings. In the preceding chapter we showed that the calm poetic voice-over provided a sharp contrast with the visual track.

The images described above do not merely provide information about what the effects of the bomb at Hiroshima were on humans and objects, but more importantly they provoke a sensation of bodily discomfort, a lived experience rather than a visual representation of Hiroshima. According to Antunes' theories, the nociceptive experience would be the result of seeing these images in a manner that exceeds mere sympathy for the pain of others. Because patients on-screen are not characters involved in the narrative, the sympathy factor would not intervene very strongly. The close-up of skins and wounds detach the image from the sufferer, annihilating any potential sympathy, but conjure a tactile sense of pain.

In *India Song*, desire is central to the film, but not its representation, as we have already seen. Viewers are drawn to the aesthetics of the image, independent of meaning creation since the narrative is not constructed through visual clues. Duras explores the potential of the image in order to create a space for contact: the close-ups of the hair, the breast, the jewellery, draw the viewer's attention close to the surface of the objects, to the rich texture of bodies and objects on-screen.

Similar to the shots of *Hiroshima mon amour* analysed above, the film encourages spectators to feel the surface of the objects and experience their tactility through the sense of vision. It is through the extreme close-ups, by bringing the objects close to the vision of spectators and by annihilating the depth of field, that the images stimulate and simulate the sense of touch.

The slow pan on the map of India in *India Song* (Figure 4.2) is another interesting example of tactility: it is not providing geographical information, but triggers a physical engagement with the image, as it has the colour and texture of flesh and looks more like an anatomical drawing of the human body than a map. The combination of pan and close-up mimics a tactile gesture over a fleshy surface and provokes a sensation rather than providing knowledge about the geography of India. The narrative does not justify a shot of this old map and it seems to be there with the only purpose of representing and inviting a sensation.

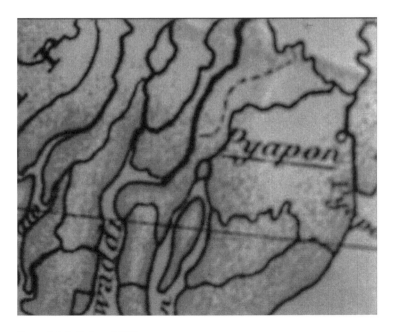

Figure 4.2 *India Song* (DVD)

Dance scenes punctuate *India Song*, a choreography of bodies, immobile or slowly moving, often in skin contact, while the voices tell of the impossibility of their relation. Richardson strokes Anne-Marie Stretter's hair, but for spectators the lived experience of touch will take place even more vividly through the close-up of her hair – so close that spectators feel as if they could smell its scent – rather than through identification with the characters on-screen.

As mentioned by McMahon in her study of *India Song*, 'the figure of the red bicycle becomes a privileged, tactile site for the unreciprocated desire of the Vice-Consul' (McMahon 2008: 200). The voices in *India Song* describe the bicycle 'this thing that she has touched', the 'inadmissible', the unrepresented intimacy spectators can only imagine via the repeated shot of the bicycle.

The close-ups – as the camera caresses the texture of the fabric of Anne-Marie Stretter's clothing, the silver necklace and the red wig, all disembodied objects (Figure 4.3) – remind us of her death. The composition of the haptic close-ups of the texture and colours of her

Figure 4.3 *India Song* (DVD)

belongings evokes desire and privileges an embodied reception for the spectators whose eyes are more like fingers caressing the disembodied objects. Hence, desire becomes a lived experience for *India Song*'s viewers rather than a process of identification with characters and narrative. As stated by Shaviro in *The Cinematic Body*:

> When I am caught up in watching a film I do not really 'identify' in the psychoanalytic sense with the activity of the (male) protagonist, or with that protagonist's gaze, or even with what theorists have called the 'omnivoyeuristic' look of the camera. It is more the case that I am brought into intimate contact with the images on screen by a process of mimesis or contagion. (Shaviro 1993: 51)

In *Césarée*, the close-ups of the carved stone of the hieroglyphics on the obelisk of the Place de la Concorde (Figure 4.4), the smooth and shiny surface of Maillol (Figure 4.5) statues, the eroded stone of female faces of statues, the metallic texture of the scaffold which imprison them (Figure 4.6), all draw attention to the surface of the objects. As spectators, we are asked to observe and feel the objects rather than make sense of them, and to remain in a pre-symbolic, prelinguistic relation with them.

Figure 4.4 *Césarée* (DVD)

Figure 4.5 *Césarée* (DVD)

Figure 4.6 *Césarée* (DVD)

The case of *Le Navire Night* is also worth mentioning for its innovative use of images, showing projectors, screen, piano, actors being made up, in fact the technical preparation of a film, a film which will not be shot. In the prologue, Duras explains that, after only two days of shooting, she was on the verge of abandoning the film, but then decided instead to film the process of filming itself, or as she put it *'tourner le désastre du film'* ('shoot the disaster of the film') (Duras et al. 1979: 15). By drawing attention to its own making, the film reveals itself in its process and materiality (Günther 2002: 45). The film provoked hostile reactions in the media, which called it *'le degré zéro de l'écriture cinématographique'* (Duras 2014a: 1666). Others saw in the film a poetics of the image and perceived common points with the paintings of Henri Michaux. For Michel Cornot, in *Le Navire Night*, 'Finally, the eyes see and touch',[1] which Dominique Noguez agrees with, adding: 'One finds in this blind film, in this love story without images, some of the most beautiful images of the entire contemporary cinema'[2] (Duras 2014a: 1667).

There is a series of haptic shots in the film including an intriguing and repetitive close-up of a red shimmering Vietnamese dress, which has no link with the story told by the voice. It illustrates what Marks indicates about haptic shots in multicultural films, that is, that they allow the image to sensuously evoke the memory of objects belonging to another culture. The gleaming red dress recurrently appears on the screen like an obsessive memory, but it is its aesthetics and tactile qualities that resurface and are transmitted to viewers through the technique of the haptic close-up.

According to Marks, the cinematic encounter takes place not only between the viewer's body and the film's body, but also between the spectator's and the film's sensoria. We bring our own personal and cultural organisation of the senses to cinema, which in turn brings a particular organisation of the senses to us, with the filmmaker's own sensorium refracting through the cinematic apparatus. One could say that the intercultural spectatorship is the meeting of two different sensoria, which may or may not intersect. Spectatorship is thus an act of sensory translation of cultural knowledge (Marks 2000: 153). Jennifer Barker explains that exploring cinema's tactility

> opens up the cinema as *intimate* experience and our relationship with cinema as a close encounter, rather than as a distant experience and observation, which the cinema as a purely visual medium presumes. To say that we are touched by cinema indicates that it has significance for us, that it comes close to us, and that it literally occupies our sphere. We share things with it: texture, spatial orientation, rhythm and vitality. (Barker 2009: 2)

Spectators are touched by Duras' films, beyond identification with characters and plots. The fragmented narratives have led some scholars to comment on her Brechtian distanciation: 'Duras deploys a series of deliberately anti-realist techniques, replacing the familiar reality effects with her own unsettling "alienation effects", reminiscent of the theatre of Bertold Brecht' (Günther 2002: 64). Paradoxically, as shown in Chapter 2, Duras succeeded in reconstructing a familiar reality around her when making films (she filmed in her house, often with the same actors, and her son had an important technical role), therefore abolishing, at least for her and those familiar with her work and life, some alienating effects. She also constructed a sense of familiarity and closeness through the recycling of unused shots, and the repetition of themes such as the water element. The tactility of her visual tracks contributes to creating an intimacy with the sensorial world of the films. Distance and intimacy are hence constantly present and characteristic of her filmic style.

Olfaction

Although it may seem that smell could not play any part in film, except by diffusing scents in the movie theatre, film theorists and neuro-scientists alike have shown that the experience of viewing a film is multisensory, and thus that the sense perceptions work jointly. Smell is a mimetic sense, and, according to Marks, 'sights may evoke smells (rising steam or smoke evokes smells of fire, incense, or cooking)' (Marks 2000: 203) through intersensory links or synaesthesia. Marks focuses one of her chapters on the sense of smell in film and suggests that smell can be conveyed in film through identification with a character smelling or sniffing, through synaesthetic links and through haptic appreciation of close-up images and images of touch. She pursues the argument that 'the sensorium is malleable, that the sense modalities work in concert, and that all sense experience is informed by culture' (Marks 2000: 203).

A long, slow shot of the wet sand in *Agatha et les lectures illimitées* or in *Nuit noire, Calcutta,* a close-up of Anne-Marie Stretter's hair, the smoke from an incense stick burning, in *India Song* all weave synaesthetic links between vision, touch and olfaction. As explained by Marks:

> We are constantly recreating the world in our bodies … Cinema by virtue of its richer and muddier semiotic relationship to the world is all the more an agent of mimesis and synesthesis than writing is … Cinema is a mimetic medium, capable of drawing us into sensory participation with its world … Images are fetishes, which the reader can translate … into sensuous experience. (Marks 2002: 214)

Smell, like touch, is a proximal sense and there is a link between proximity and olfaction as the closer we get to the source of smell the stronger the smell gets. 'The close-up encourages the viewer to extend their sensorium and to draw on the proximal senses that might otherwise be kept at bay' (Elliott 2011: 129). For Marks, the experience of being in another's culture drives the desire to appeal to proximity and embodied knowledge, and the appeal to smell is one way that intercultural and diasporic identity can be established. In Duras' films, not only do the images conjure tactility, they also link to the sense of olfaction and participate in the re-creation of a fragmented sensory world: the smell of the sea, of wet sand, of hair, of skin and of incense. The voice, as we will see in the next chapter, will also contribute to triggering olfaction through the vocative power of words and their poetic function rather than close-olfactory haptics, to use Elliott's term.

Water, light and thermoception

Water is a central element of Duras' films, *une image passe-partout* (a master image), as she explains in *Green Eyes* (Duras 1990: 70), as it can signify the Seine, the Ganges or the Mekong. It functions as a mirroring effect and can refract the sea of *Un barrage contre le Pacifique*, the Ganges of *Nuit noire, Calcutta* or the Mekong of *L'Amant*. Duras mentioned its importance on numerous occasions in interviews.

The presence of the water element has been read by critics as having the effect of facilitating the spectators' regression towards an archaic maternal space, as the film's visual track puts us in a trance-like state,

Figure 4.7 *Nuit noire, Calcutta* (DVD)

generating an increased receptiveness to the soothing quality of Duras' language and of her voice (Heinrich 1980: 46). With its shimmering surfaces and light reflections, water gives rise to numerous shots of exquisite beauty, as is the case in Duras' first co-authored film, *Nuit noire, Calcutta* (directed by Marin Karmitz, 1964) (Figure 4.7) or of more recent films like *La Femme du Gange, Agatha et les lectures illimitées, L'Homme atlantique* and *Aurélia Steiner (Melbourne)*.

These shots emphasise the movements of the water, its reflective qualities and its glistening colours, while the beaches and sand banks add grainy textures (Figures 4.8 and 4.9) to the liquid space.

There is little or no relation with the stories told by the voices, although such shots fill up most of the screen time. They allow for an aesthetic experience of sensations associated with the water element, not solely at the visual level but as an entire bodily experience. Gallese explains the multimodality of vision:

> Neuroscience has shown that vision is multimodal: it encompasses the activation of motor, somatosensory, and emotion-related brain networks. Motor neurons not only cause movements and actions but they also respond to body-related visual, tactile,

Figure 4.8 *Nuit noire, Calcutta* (DVD)

Figure 4.9 *Nuit noire, Calcutta* (DVD)

and auditory stimuli, mapping the space around us, the objects
at hand in that very same space, and the actions of others.
(Gallese 2017b: 7)

Long shots of the surface of the water in *Aurélia Steiner (Melbourne)*,
for example, stimulate spectators' many senses: thermoception, as well
as senses of movement, time, space and smell. In many cases the shots
are of long duration which intensifies their sensorial impact on viewers,
imprinting the viewers' bodies.

Camera movement and the vestibular sense

Camera movements are considered to be a key element in the intersub-
jective relation between viewer and screen. In their article on the feeling
of motion in cinema, Vittorio Gallese and Michele Guerra promote 'an
embodied approach to camera movements . . . by analysing their effects
on viewers' motor cortex activation' (Gallese and Guerra 2014: 104).
They point out that camera movements contribute to the style of a film
because

> style is basically what strengthens our relationship with a work of
> art, what allows us to orient (or lose) ourselves within the imaginary
> world of fiction. Style is a way to manipulate the mediation, to
> establish a peculiar intersubjective relation between the work of
> art and us. (Gallese and Guerra 2014: 104)

Vivian Sobchack (1982: 317) identifies four basic kinds of movement
in moving pictures: the movement of actors and objects within the
frame, the movement between images produced by editing, the movement from a static position of the camera such as the pan or the zoom,
and the tracking shots where the whole camera moves. In Duras'
films, movements are very reduced: characters are often still or move
very slowly as if in a dream state, editing is limited with no flashback
techniques, fade in and out and zooms are inexistent, but slow tracking
shots are present in all the films and often without diegetic justification.
The shots alternate between a still camera remaining on an object or an
actor for an extended time and a slow-moving camera often combined
with a long sequence shot. In *Le Camion*, half of the visual track is made

of tracking shots taken mostly from the cabin of the lorry. The tracking shots of urban and suburban flat landscapes resemble those of the water in *Nuit noire, Calcutta, Aurélia Steiner (Melbourne), Agatha et les lectures illimtées, L'Homme atlantique* and *La Femme du Gange*. They are always slow travelling shots, of a scarcely if at all populated landscape not linked to the narrative. In *Le Camion*, the abundance of those slow camera movements is punctuated by still shots of the inside of the reading room where Duras and Depardieu read the scenario of the film. This rhythm creates in spectators a hypnotic feeling, a sense of enrapture typical of Duras' filmic style.

With their very slow pace, stillness, slowly flowing narratives, long takes and long silences that make time palpable and elongate it, Duras' films could be thought to be the precursors of 'slow cinema', a contemporary genre of cinema based on 'the employment of (often extremely) long takes, decentred and understated modes of storytelling, and a pronounced emphasis on quietude and the everyday' (Flanagan 2008). It is a type of filmmaking that is, like Duras' films, minimalist, contemplative with little narrative and that compels us to 'retreat from a culture of speed, modifies our expectations of filmic narration' (Flanagan 2008). Like 'slow cinema', Duras' films provide spectators with a different lived experience of time and movement perception.

In their analysis of the effects of camera movements on spectators, Gallese and Guerra explain:

> While the still camera can provide a strong impression of reality but does not reduce the distance between the viewer and the screen, the moving camera not only implements our experience by adding kinaesthetic, bodily, tactile cues as well as a sense of balance and gravity, but also gives the impression that the movie is to some extent *live*, that there is an intentionality which endows it with peculiar bodily functions and subjectivity. (Gallese and Guerra 2014: 106)

In their discussion on the reasons why a filmmaker would use camera movements, Gallese and Guerra suggest that when the camera moves, spectators are given additional information about the space being filmed as well as a sense of being there (Gallese and Guerra 2014: 107). The effect produced is embodied, as viewers have the sense of moving to discover the space and feel as if they were moving in space (Sobchack

1982: 317). While Duras' filmic narratives are fragmented and do not provide a strong reality effect for spectators, as already mentioned, this is compensated by the use of numerous slow camera pans and tracking shots which create a particular bodily kinaesthetic effect, a languor, a sense of lassitude and lethargy which clearly mimics characters' behaviours when present on-screen as can be seen in *Nathalie Granger*, *Baxter, Vera Baxter* and *India Song*.

Antunes has identified the vestibular sense as one of the additional senses to the five senses. He defines it as 'our capacity to navigate in space' and asserts that: 'Although we are in a seated position, the vestibular shapes our perceptual experience of a film at all times' (Antunes 2016: loc. 1162). While tracking shots do contribute to our sense of navigation in space, the vestibular sense is a multisensorial one in which sound has an important role to play. For instance, the soundtrack might produce exterior sounds, such as a dog barking or birds singing, while the mobile camera of the visual track shows the inside of the Château Rothschild in *India Song*. As we have shown, not only does the desynchronisation compound the vestibular effect, but it also provides contradictory spatial signals of proximity (indoor noise) and distance and even remoteness.

Mirrors and disorientation

The presence of the mirror is a leitmotiv in Duras' films on which much has been written by Duras scholars, but I would like to suggest the idea that the mirror in *Agatha et les lectures illimitées* and *India Song* in particular affects spectators' vestibular sense by disorientating them. Mirror shots prevent the easy recognition of the filmic space, problematise the framing by blurring the distinction between in and out of frame as well as the notions of on- and off-screen, thus creating a feeling of spatial and filmic disorientation. Broken mirrors in *Son nom de Venise dans Calcutta désert* further problematise spatial orientation, which is confirmed by the female voice asking: 'Where are we?'

The mirror disturbs the sense of space between spectator and image, since it is a surface that reflects but has no real depth; it constructs an illusionary dimension in which spectators lose their sense of spatial reality and orientation. While there is no narrative justification for filming in the mirror, it forges a relationship of distrust between image and viewer, who does not know what to expect regarding the movement of actors in and out of frame and through the framed space. The film suture, a technique used to make us forget that it is the camera that is really doing the looking, is also affected. Mulvey (1975) has argued there are three looks implied by film: the look of the camera itself; the look of the audience watching the film; and the look of the characters on-screen. In traditional cinema, we are invited to identify with the look of the male characters so that we forget the mechanical look of the camera and our own invested look at the screen. The mirror in Duras' films problematises the three looks as we become aware of the camera angle and confused about who is looking and what characters are looking at. In *L'Homme atlantique* and *Le Camion*, the camera, breaking all the taboos, is even reflected in the glass of the window. The vestibular sense is challenged by the slow track shots, interrupted by still shots, and by the incoherent mirror reflections. While spectators are immobile their sense of locomotion and movement is activated by the movement of visual images, the wandering motion of the actors, or even their static position as they lean against walls or windows, which in the absence of a linked narrative, reduces cinema to its very specificity: a moving image that impacts on the vestibular and kinaesthetic sense of its viewers.

The colour blue and sensorial memories

According to Duras scholar Anne Cousseau, 'Colour is the means by which one can reach pure affect and by which the immediate encounter with the physical world takes place'[3] (Cousseau 2002: 39). Elliott explains that Merleau-Ponty likens the experience of colour to that of falling asleep: we do not enter sleep before it becomes us – we are sleep. There is a corporeal aspect to colour that invades our bodies as soon as we are presented with it (Elliott 2011: 59). This is important in cinema as we sit in the dark and we are presented with images saturated with colours. The body's corporeal response to colours is a major part of how we react to the film.

Duras has revealed the importance of the colour blue carried along by images of the blue water, the Mekong, the sea and the sky of her childhood. In *The Lover*, she writes:

> I can't really remember the days. The light of the sun blurred and annihilated all colour. But the nights, I remember them. The blue was more distant than the sky, beyond all depths, covering the bounds of the world. The sky, for me, was the stretch of brilliance crossing the blue that coal coalescence beyond all colours … The air was blue, you could hold it in your hand. Blue. The sky was a continual throbbing of the brilliance of the light. (Duras 2006: loc. 860)

The colour blue is presented in *The Lover* as an essential element of the sensorial memories of her childhood including early aesthetic experience. It is also dominant in seascapes of, among other films, *Agatha et les lectures illimitées* (Figures 4.10 and 4.11). Although the film is not directly linked to those childhood memories, the liquid blue pervades the entire film including the final shot of a painting from an unknown painter (Figure 4.12). Gilles Deleuze points out that a liquid quality increasingly marks the visual image in Duras' films and that: 'Cinematographically, Marguerite Duras can be compared to a great painter who might say: if only I could manage to capture a wave, just a

Figure 4.10 *Agatha et les lectures illimitées* (DVD)

Figure 4.11 *Agatha et les lectures illimitées* (DVD)

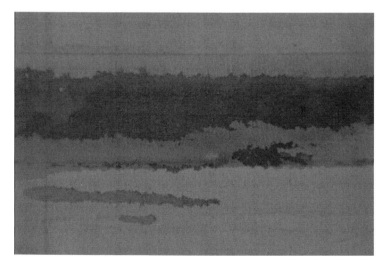

Figure 4.12 *Agatha et les lectures illimitées* (DVD)

wave, or a bit of wet sand' (Deleuze 1989: 258). What Duras attempts to capture in her films is the sensorial element of colour as described in *The Lover* and associated with childhood: it combines the colour blue and the gleaming of the sea.

Figure 4.13 *Aurélia Steiner (Vancouver)* (DVD)

In black and white films, such as *Aurélia Steiner (Vancouver)*, the shots of the rocks emphasise their 'brillance' as they are swept by the sea (Figure 4.13) and contrast with the dull grey of the concrete of the blockhouses.

Film after film, Duras attempts to capture the sensorial experience of a spectacle of her childhood as described in *The Lover*, repeating the same shots with slight variations and refinement as if always dissatisfied with the results. What the colours and light reconstruct is a poetics of sensations that elicit and affect the viewers' senses.[4] The lack of characters on-screen and the pace of the films lead spectators to contemplation and heighten their receptivity as if in front of a painting.

Tableaux vivants, 'nudes' and black screens

As Deleuze (1989: 259) remarks, Duras as a filmmaker can be compared to a painter, and many of her film shots are like *tableaux vivants* or *plans-tableaux*, with motifs and figures such as the landscapes we have already seen and the nudes. In *India Song* and *Baxter, Vera Baxter*, the composition and framing of the naked bodies of Delphine Seyrig (Figure 4.14) and Claudine Gabay (Figure 4.15) focus on the breasts of

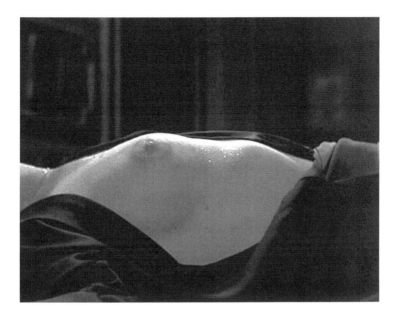

Figure 4.14 *India Song* (DVD)

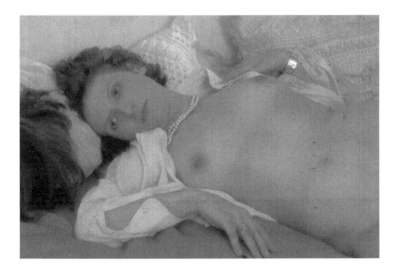

Figure 4.15 *Baxter, Vera Baxter* (DVD)

the two women, the fleshy texture, the grain of the skin, its colour and even the droplets of perspiration which can be seen on Seyrig's skin. The shots foreground the haptic quality of the experience rather than a voyeuristic gaze, partly because of the intimacy of the close-up, partly because both shots are long and static.

Without narrative or related plot, but visually striking, they are simultaneously abstract and sensual, and require from viewers an attitude of aesthetic contemplation more akin to watching a painting than a film. They are like *tableaux vivants* with an excess of realism in the reproduction of the motif and an excess of haptic elements.

While movement, colours and light play an important role in the poetics of sense perceptions, the black screen is a recurrent motif in Duras' films that has given rise to a number of interpretations. In her early films, it is linked to the diegesis and is an important structural device in *Les Mains négatives*, *Césarée*, *Aurélia Steiner (Melbourne)*, *Aurélia Steiner (Vancouver)* and *Agatha et les lectures illimitées*. A careful examination of the films shows that the number of black images or almost black images (Figure 4.16) increases with each film as if Duras was experimenting with how far she could go in the filmic transgression represented by a black screen. In our previous chapter we remarked on the progression from voice-over to desynchronisation as a sign that Duras was slowly daring to subvert the cinematographic medium. Similarly, the black

Figure 4.16 *Aurélia Steiner (Melbourne)* (DVD)

screen becomes increasingly independent from the story being told and reaches the point where black shots take up twenty-five minutes of screen time in *L'Homme atlantique*.

While it has been interpreted as a destructive gesture, an act of annihilation of representation, I have argued that it is also the representation of Duras' understanding of the origin of feminine writing and creativity: the 'organic night' or the 'dark shadow' as she called it (Royer 2009).

Duras said of *L'Homme atlantique* that it was her last film and that even if she continued to make films, *L'Homme atlantique* would be her last (Duras 2014b: 937). It is a paradoxical statement that highlights the importance she gave to the film as the one that had finally accomplished the total destruction of film conventions. She became aware she could not go any further in the subversion of the film medium after *L'Homme atlantique*. She directed another two films after that: *Il Dialoguo di Roma* (1982) and *Les Enfants* (1984), but they do not reach the degree of filmic transgression of *L'Homme atlantique*.

I would like to suggest a new interpretation of the black screen and will do so by linking the film to the work of Pierre Soulages' famous series of black canvasses, which he titled *Outrenoir* and exhibited in 1979 at the Pompidou Centre in Paris. His coming to the black paintings is hence contemporary to Duras' film *L'Homme atlantique* (1981). He explains the process that led him to *Outrenoir*:

> I thought it was bad. But I continued working on it for two or three hours because I felt that it would become somehow stronger if I kept working on it. Eventually I went to sleep, and a few hours later I looked at what I had done. I was no longer working in black but working with the light reflected by the surface of the black. The light was dynamized by the strokes of paint. It was another world. (Soulages in Heyman 2014)

Soulages adds that the colour black taps into something basic, human and timeless: 'Black is the colour of the origin of painting – and our own origin. In French, we say the baby "sees the day", to mean he was born. Before that, of course, we were in the dark' (Soulages in Heyman 2014). Similarly, for Duras the black screen is the origin of creativity, of writing and of cinema, the 'organic night' that precedes and contains all the images and written texts (Royer 2009: 163). The black screen exemplifies the process of writing which for Duras consists in 'being engulfed in the internal shadow which drowns, which dies in the light of clear memory and one day spills out, there, before us[5] (Duras 2014a: 326).

Similarly to Soulages' discovery of black paint, Duras gave an account of her discovery of the black screen as being coincidental and not a conscious act:

> A significant event happened with *L'Homme atlantique*. I didn't have enough unused shots from *Agatha et les lectures illimitées* to complete the film. And I didn't want to fill it with images shot just for this reason ... I wanted to keep the film incomplete ... So, I used black shots, many ... After ten minutes of black screen, it was done, it was inconceivable to find images to fill in the film.[6] (Duras 1981: 30)

According to Samuel Challéat, in a discussion of Soulages' *Outrenoir* and the reaction of viewers:

> Placed in front of those large canvasses, the spectator is engulfed in the space they create, struck by the intensity of their presence. A physical presence, tactile, sensuous, which exudes a formidable contained energy. But it is also metaphysical, which encourages interiority and mediation. A painting with a powerful silent materiality ... (Benos and Challéat 2014)

For Duras, the black screen can be scratched, damaged like an image can be. She says that what distinguishes the black screen is that

> it can reflect the shadows that pass in front of it, like water or glass can. What we can see emerge on the black are glimmers, shapes, people who pass in front of the cabin, things that have been forgotten in the windows of the cabin, and shapes that cannot be identified, essentially ocular, appearing suddenly from the immensity of the restful state of the eyes created by the black, or on the contrary the fright that comes to some when we suggest that they look without anything to look at. Rivers, lakes, oceans have the power of black images.[7] (Duras 2014b: 928)

Both Duras and Soulages experiment with their respective mediums and peel off the meanings of their work to reach the medium's materiality where representation is no longer necessary: the black screen and the black canvas belong to the same experimentation with the materiality of the medium they work with. Confronted by the density of the blackness of the screen, the spectator stumbles against the impenetrable and mysterious matter of the film. The effect of the black screen on Duras' spectators is even more pronounced than in *Outrenoir* because the sound track immerses spectators in an auditory envelope while the screen, an oversized painting, captures their gaze.

As is the case for *Outrenoir*, Duras' spectators can no longer be absorbed by the meaning of the film at an intellectual level, but are engaged in a perceptual, sensorial experience. Pierre Soulages recommended that spectators look at his black canvasses with their eyes and not with the word 'black' in their mind, reminding spectators that a painting, even covered with black, aims at the senses of spectators rather than at their intellect (Benos and Challéat 2014). This captures the essence of Duras' work on the visual track, which aims first at our senses and is a multimodal aesthetic response, combining not only sound and image but also text and painting.

Duras has experimented with visuality more than is recognised by scholars. She has recreated throughout her films sensorial worlds echoing embodied childhood memories of spaces, colours, light, touch, smells, temperature and kinaesthesis. This sensorial world cannot, however, be detached from female subjectivity. Art is a crucial means of expression and communication for women allowing them to enter into relationships and to cultivate their sensorial perceptions through creative imagination (Bolton 2011: 193). This creativity must work 'not only with words but also with colours and sounds as possible matters to represent, communicate and sublimate fleshly energy and attraction' (Irigaray 2004a: 99). Duras' films offer spectators a new and different visual engagement with the medium. It bears no similarities with Mulvey's criticism of the visuality of mainstream cinema, as they are giving access to a multisensorial world that resonates with Duras' own female experience with interculturality.

Understanding how particular film techniques can embody or re-embody our female experience is therefore useful in order to answer the question posed in this book: how do Duras' films express her female subjectivity and involve viewers? The next chapter will pursue the same question, but by focusing on the soundtrack. How does the soundtrack which has primacy over the visual track in her films encourage listeners to perceive otherwise, and what is the specificity of that listening to female voices and laughter, male cries, music and sound effects?

Notes

1   (My translation) 'Enfin, les yeux voient et touchent.'
2   (My translation) 'On trouve dans ce film d'aveugles, dans cette histoire d'amour sans images, quelques-unes des plus belles images de tout le cinéma contemporain.'
3   (My translation)'La couleur est la voie par laquelle on atteint l'affect pur, [la voie] par laquelle s'effectue la rencontre immédiate avec le monde sensible.'
4   I am indebted to Carol Murphy who presented a paper on the topic of colours in Duras' texts, 'La Couleur des Mots: Sensations colorantes dans des textes de Marguerite Duras', presented at the conference 'Duras and the Arts' (Sydney, 2016).
5   (My translation) 'L'engouffrement dans l'ombre interne, qui s'y noie, qui meurt à la mémoire claire et puis, qui un jour, sort là, devant nous'.
6   (My translation) 'Un événement considérable est survenu avec *L'Homme atlantique*. Je n'avais pas assez de chutes d'*Agatha et les lectures illimitées* pour le remplir d'images. Et je ne voulais pas le remplir d'images tournées pour ça, pour lui, pour lui donner son plein d'images. Je voulais le garder tel quel insuffisant . . . Alors j'ai employé du noir, beaucoup . . . Au bout de dix minutes de noir, c'était fait, il était devenu inconcevable de trouver une image sur ce texte'.
7   (My translation) 'c'est qu'il peut refléter les ombres qui passent devant lui, comme l'eau, la vitre. Ce qu'on voit parfois subvenir sur le noir ce sont des lueurs, des formes, des gens qui passent dans la cabine, des appareils oubliés dans les fenêtres de la cabine, et des formes non identifiables, purement oculaires, surgies de l'immensité du repos des yeux créée par le noir, ou bien au contraire, de l'épouvante qui devrait venir à certains quand on leur propose de regarder sans leur proposer d'objet à voir. Les cours d'eau, les lacs, les océans ont la puissance des images noires.'

5

Soundscape: sonic aesthetics and the feminine

> The aural boundaries between body and world may feel indistinct: the rustle of trees mingles with the sound of my breathing, conversely the booming music may inhabit my chest cavity and move my body from the inside. (Marks 2000: 183)

Duras' films, and in particular the films of the Indian cycle, rely heavily on the power of their sonic elements: the human voice – which speaks, sings, laughs and shouts – the music, the silence and the sound effects. Duras scholars who have written on sound have, however, essentially focused on the projected sound and its meaning. Studies of sound centre on the monologues and dialogues of the voice-over, which are often treated as literary scripts, as a means of understanding the narrative. This chapter proposes to approach the question of the sonic elements not only from the point of view of their relevance to the films and the narratives, but also from the perspective of the received sound, that is, from the point of view of the acoustic spectator. Duras' soundtracks are often complex orchestrations that provoke and promote the active participation of spectators' imagination and embodied reception. In this section of the book, I will explore the significance of the non-semantic vocalisations and their capacity to engage us sensuously. I will focus on two main questions: how does Duras, as a female filmmaker, use sound to instil a particular experience in the audience? How can her use of sound be linked to female subjectivity? To do so, after a theoretical introduction on the function and effects of cinematic sound, I will consider all the sonic elements that compose Duras' soundtracks.

Pudovkin, Eisenstein and Alexandrov, even before the beginnings of sound film, commented on the use of sound in cinema:

> The first experimental work with sound must be directed along the line of its distinct non-synchronisation with the visual images. And only such an attack will give the necessary palpability, which will later lead to the creation of an orchestral counterpoint of visual and aural images. (Pudovkin et al. 1985: 84)

Contrary to what they recommended, as soon as filmic sound became available, filmmakers used it to complement the image and quickly established a relation of dependence between sound and image. Chion remarks on the status of sound in mainstream cinema:

> Ontologically speaking, and historically too, film sound is considered as a 'plus', an add-on. The underlying discourse goes like this: even though the cinema was endowed with synchronous sound after thirty years of perfectly good existence without it, whose soundtrack in recent years has become ever richer, crackling and pulsating, even now the cinema has kept its ontologically visual definition no less intact. A film without sound remains a film; a film with no image, or at least without a visual frame for projection, is not a film. (Chion 1994: 143)

Film sound has been used to unify and bind the flow of images, and provide unity using non-diegetic music and synchronised dialogues. It is commonly used to serve the visual track and the narrative, and seldom as an independent feature of the film. It has therefore always been perceived as a background element and, for a long time, received poor scrutiny from film theorists. However, studies by film theorist Michel Chion brought a new 'visibility' to sound with his seminal work *Audio-Vision* (1994). Craig Sinclair's 'Audition: Making Sense of/in the Cinema' also shows the 'sublime power of sound within cinema' (Sinclair 2003: 17) and its potential for a 'sonic equivalent of Laura Mulvey's (male) gaze' (Sinclair 2003: 17). Although sound is often ignored, it is also very present, due to its natural factors, as we are never free from the imperative to hear, we are always immersed in sound because of the 'absence of anything like eyelids for the ears, the omnidirectionality of hearing, and the physical nature of sound'

(Chion 1994: 33). Unlike the image, sound has no boundaries: although it often seems to emanate from the screen or the character, 'it extends beyond the bounds of its apparatus and invades the space of the listener' (Elliott 2011: 153).

Duras' films, whether they are synchronised or desynchronised, give sound a greater place and function than is reserved for it in mainstream cinema. In her synchronised films (*Détruire dit-elle, Jaune le soleil, Nathalie Granger*), voices, silences and music have the narrative primacy over the visual track, which shows, as we have mentioned in our previous chapter, slow-moving characters, actors lacking any physical expression and shots of empty rooms. These films undermine the traditional hegemony of the visual and challenge the assumed power, superiority and supremacy of the image. This subversion of the film apparatus is pursued further with *La Femme du Gange*, Duras' first desynchronised film, followed by *India Song, Son nom de Venise dans Calcutta désert* and several other films, using the same technique. By breaking the connection between sight and hearing and subverting synchronicity, the films show the power of sound to the audience, independent of images, and spectators used to gazing at the screen to glean information have to switch their perception from the ocular to the auditory in an effort to make sense of the narrative.

What is the effect of such emphasis on hearing when we know that sound greatly affects the body? According to sound engineer David Sonnenschein, who studied the physical reception of sound, which he calls the 'sound energy transformation' (Sonnenschein 2001: xxii), sound has a powerful, unmediated effect on the body:

> Sound can affect your body temperature, blood circulation, pulse rate, breathing, and sweating. Loud music with a strong beat can raise body heat, while soft, floating, or detached abstract music can lower it, noise can energise, release pain and dissipate tension. (Sonnenschein 2001: 71)

Not only does sound carry meaning, triggers memory and speaks to our mind, in film it can have a primary effect outside any process of identification with characters. Elliott suggests that our subjective reactions to sound may be the result of a biological and neurological reception rather than the other way around:

> In other words, our bodies here are working in a way that is exactly opposite to many notions of film theory that assume our heart beats faster because we experience the emotional content of a film rather than our bodies receiving corporeal stimulation in the form of sound waves. (Elliott 2011: 146)

As explained by Anna Powell in the context of her studies on horror films, 'sound waves, as well as light waves, travel through us and work strongly on the sensorium, bypassing the cerebral cortex and mainlining into our central nervous system' (Powell 2006: 206), confirming the role of the body in the process of the reception of sounds.

This is an important point, since in Duras' films there is no attempt to create characters' psychology or to produce an identification process between spectators and characters. The audience's reaction comes from the corporeal effects of cinema in which sound has a privileged position.

After this brief introduction, let us now examine the sonic elements, starting with the voice, which, in the hierarchy of sounds defined by Dominique Chateau, is at the top:

> At the top, there are the words, able to challenge the image because of their semantic and structural richness. At the centre, sound effects, destined to comply with the instructions of the diegesis, represented by the image. At the bottom, music, simple creator of the atmosphere of the film.[1] (Chateau 1976: 91)

The voice

Although the voice is considered to be the major element of the soundtrack, it is considered so because of its capacity to create meaning, as explained by Chateau. For Schaeffer (1946a), on the contrary, the spoken word should be treated as a raw sonic element rather than as a cohesive text to be declaimed by actors.

Voices in Duras' films, especially those of the Indian cycle, *Navire Night*, the *Aurélia Steiner* films, *Agatha* and *L'Homme atlantique* have no visual representation and fit with Chion's definition of *acousmêtre*:

> When the acousmatic presence is a voice, and especially when this voice has not yet been visualised – that is when we cannot yet

connect it to a face – we get a special being, a kind of talking and acting shadow to which we attach the name *acousmêtre*. (Chion 1999: 19–21)

These occurrences of *acousmêtre* are supposed to have the responsibility of narrating the story, but in Duras' films the narration is fragmented, incoherent, often contradictory, and while the role of *acousmêtre* is essential to the film, it is not only for semantic reasons. The language used does not follow the rules of grammar, expected intonation and logic: sentences are often elliptical and contain a great number of nouns and very few verbs, thus creating a feeling of confusion in a disconcerted audience used to more active and structured sentences. According to Barthes (1975), sentences are hierarchical, they imply subjections, subordinations, and domineering elements such as verbs, but in Duras' films, they are dismantled, open, with an accumulation of passive grammar elements which mime the passivity of the actors on-screen and is transmitted to the listeners.

The intonation of the voices rarely follows the normal pattern of a drop at the end of the sentence or a slight rise as if a question was being asked or there is uncertainty in the statement. The delivery is slow and hesitant with many pauses and silences that interrupt the flow, leaving spectators unsure about what is really happening in the story.

The dialogues and monologues have poetic qualities: associations between words are provided by rhymes, alliterations, assonances, metaphors, rather than by logically constructed sentences. There are many examples of such qualities in all the films, but the dialogues of *India Song* and *Son nom de Venise dans Calcutta désert* present very clear examples of the poetic function of the voices, as shown in the following example from *India Song*:

- cette lumière (that light)
- la mousson (the monsoon)
- cette poussière (that dust)
- Calcutta central (central Calcutta)
- Il y a comme une odeur de fleur? (the smell of flowers?)
- la lèpre (leprosy)
- Où est-on? (Where are we?)

These dialogues display a predominance of noun phrases, play on sounds (such as the rhymes *lumière* (light) and *poussière* (dust)), pauses and silences, creating an unusual poetic dimension. The piano music theme in the background reinforces the poetic function of the dialogues.

The texture and cadence of the voices, with their slow delivery of the text, emphasise the sonorities, the timbre and resonance of the words and, as in poetry, the voices have a synaesthetic power. In the example above, olfaction (smell of flowers), feeling of humidity (monsoon), dryness (dust) and luminosity (that light), intertwine to create a synaesthetic and embodied experience of an imaginary Calcutta, and a cinaesthetic encounter between film and spectator. As suggested by Laine and Strauven:

> Cinesthetic encounters are based on experiencing, embodying, making sense of, and being affected by the film, in and through 'the flesh' rather than on notions of identification, visual pleasure, or the satisfaction of narrative desire. In other words, the concept of synaesthesia provides an alternative way of approaching cinematic modes of representation as a shared existence that can be found neither 'outside' in the realm of cinema, nor 'inside' in the realm of spectator, but in the textures of sensual operations between the inside and the outside. (Laine and Strauven 2009: 252)

In their recent study of cinema, Bolton and Bainbridge's use of Irigaray's theories on the feminine leads to a rethinking of our understanding of the voices in the context of studies on multisensoriality. Irigaray's proposition on what a feminine syntax could be is in many ways relevant to our study of Duras' cinema. As explained by the fact that Irigaray's *Speculum of the Other Woman* and *This Sex Which Is Not One* are contemporary with Duras' filmic experimentation, the disembodied voices have characteristics which can be very closely linked to Irigaray's description of a feminine syntax. She writes:

> What a feminine syntax might be is not simple or easy to state, because in that 'syntax' there would no longer be either subject or object, 'oneness' would no longer be privileged, there would be no proper meanings, proper names, 'proper' attributes ...

> Instead, that 'syntax' would involve nearness, proximity, but in such an extreme form it would preclude distinction of identities, any establishment of ownership, thus any form of appropriation. (Irigaray 1985b: 134)

In this statement, it is easy to recognise the characteristics of all the voices of Duras' films and in particular those of *Agatha*, *L'Homme atlantique*, *Aurélia Steiner (Melbourne)* and *India Song*: their multiplicity, the absence of clearly identifiable speakers, the disrupted syntax and the passivity and corporeal effects of Duras' syntax.

Sinclair (2003) has linked the proximate quality of voices – the spectators hear without mediation – to Irigaray's concept of the feminine that involves proximity, touch, closeness and sensuality as a way to undermine the distance of patriarchal expression and hegemony of the visual. Kristeva's study of the archaic dimension of language in *Revolution of Poetic Language* (1984), which she calls 'the semiotic', is also relevant to this study of voices. The semiotic is linked to the bodily contact between mother and child before the paternal order of language comes to separate subject and mother and is given free play in works of art. According to Kristeva, the poetic dimension of language is disruptive of the symbolic patriarchal order and is associated with musicality and rhythm. In Duras' films, the semiotic dimension as a poetic and disruptive force is given primacy over the symbolic, likened by Kristeva to the law, structure, order and the masculine. Kristeva's work had a strong influence on 1970s feminists, and her notions of 'semiotic' and 'symbolic' had an impact on the arts of the time. Duras' comments on language in the interviews *Woman to Woman* are at times very close to Irigaray and Kristeva's theories, as shown below:

> MD: I'm never concerned about the sense or the meaning. If there's sense, it shows afterward. Anyway, it's never a concern . . .
> MD: The words count more than the syntax. More than anything, it follows, at a distance. (Duras and Gauthier 1987: I)

Duras' films ask spectators to question conventional spectatorial be-haviours as representing dominant patriarchal models. Viewers have to become attentive auditors and practise what Pierre Schaeffer called 'reduced listening' (Chion 1994: 28) by focusing on the materiality of the voice rather than on the semantic codes. As explained by Chion: 'The emotional, physical, and aesthetic value of a sound is linked not only to the causal explanation we attribute to it but also to its own qualities of timbre and texture, to its own personal vibration' (Chion 1994: 31).

In the context of gender film theory, as we have already mentioned, Mulvey's (1975) seminal work on the male gaze in cinema – contemporary with Duras' film experimentations – considered the film as an entirely visual experience. The hegemony of the look as a masculine experience in cinema is clearly challenged by Duras' experimentation on the voices, which shows the extent of her visionary perspective. According to Mulvey, the female spectator is alienated from her sense of sight by the gaze and its related patriarchal appropriation (Sinclair 2003: 24). As we have seen in the chapter on visuality, Duras' visual tracks provide a different visual experience in which women and the feminine are no longer excluded. Her films also open a space for female subjectivity to be expressed and perceived through an innovative sonic experience. The visual perception no longer dominates, voices challenge it, establishing a horizontal relation between the two perceptions rather than a vertical, hierarchical one.

With the publication of Davina Quinlivan's book *The Place of Breath in Cinema* (2012), scholars in film studies have shown an increasing interest in the study of breathing in cinema. Quinlivan's study draws heavily on Luce Irigaray's (1999, 2004b) analysis of breathing as it offers her new ways in which to 'question the nature of seeing, perceiving and sensing things which are not always entirely visible in film' (Quinlivan 2012: 1). According to Quinlivan, the notion of breathing is also a venue for thinking the dynamic exchanges between inside and outside, ocular and auditory, the body and the voice that breathes air on- and off-screen, and the spectator who breathes a film through its images and sounds and their own body. Thus, it has a place in our study of embodied spectatorship in Duras' films, especially in relation to the voices. A special issue of *Music, Sound, and the Moving Image* is devoted to breath and the body of the voice in cinema. The articles explore 'the significance of "non-semantic" vocalisations related to breathing, such as sighing, gasping, sobbing, shouting, screaming, and laughing' (Garwood and Green 2016: 105) through the different phases of the film experience. In the following sections, attention will be given to some of these non-semantic vocal sounds based on breath, its suspension and its various outbursts, starting with the beggar's song of *India Song*.

India Song and *Son nom de Venise dans Calcutta désert* open with the voice of the beggar woman singing in an oriental language. The voice stops, breathes, starts laughing, then talks in the same oriental language. The semantic function of language is rendered ineffective, at least for the French ear, but its material characteristics are emphasised. The sonorities, the rhythm, the intonation, the pitch, the breathing pauses and what Barthes called 'the grain of the voice' are all we hear from the beggar, and these characteristics become the distinctive traits by which this woman, with no screen representation, is identified in the rest of the films. The beggar remains a disembodied voice throughout and comes back repeatedly, haunting the soundtrack and provoking each time in spectators an eerie feeling, disturbing and mysterious. The invisibility of the beggar, the long pauses between the foreign utterances, the uncanny laughter and the songs contribute to the spectators' embodied reactions. These types of vocalisations are not background noises but are aural close-ups that have an aural hapticity which for Marks is linked to experiences of intercultural filmmakers and allows diasporic viewers renewed contact with memories and homeplaces they have often left behind (Marks 2000: 183). The beggar's breathing can be heard through the pauses and vocalisations, paradoxically highlighting her invisible body. Quinlivan considers breathing as an '(in)visible' dimension of the human body which calls attention to the way in which boundaries of visibility and invisibility become blurred (Quinlivan 2012: 3). The voice of the beggar and other voices off-screen make the question of (in)visibility even more complex as some of the characters have no clear screen presence, but they do have aural visibility and even a strong aural presence, and thus they doubly blur the distinction between visible and invisible.

The beggar expresses in her language what Cixous (1991) considered the most important aspects of feminine writing: the vocal, the musical, language at its most archaic level. From the beginning and throughout the films, the beggar assumes a negative function: she has no visual representation, cannot be understood and is described by other voices as insane, sterile and of unknown origin. By never appearing on-screen, she is also on the side of what is normally overlooked in film apparatus and in film theory. But like the women in *Nathalie Granger*, the beggar's voice by its effects on auditory spectators permeates all layers of the film and regains agency.

According to the published scenario of the films, the beggar's voice speaks in an unknown language, 'Hindustani'. Because of the theme of the film and narrative clues, Western spectators assume that the beggar speaks in an Indian language whereas she, in fact, speaks in the Laotian language, a living language from the south of Laos. Savannakhet is the only recognisable word. My research (Royer 2014: 194–5) has shown that the beggar's song of *India Song* and *Son nom de Venise dans Calcutta désert* was very popular in Laos in the early 1940s and was a children's song, not, as suggested by several researchers, a lullaby. It is a nationalistic song expressing nostalgia and yearning for a return to the home country, Laos, through images of the lotus flower, and the sweet smell of frangipani. It is a song about memories of scents and places, which can easily be associated with Duras' own nostalgia for her childhood. The voice has uncanny oriental connotations for the French ear and provokes a feeling of otherness, whereas for Duras, Vietnamese or Laotian spectators, the experience would be, of course, one of familiarity.

The reason why Duras chose this song remains unknown, but considering her Indochinese childhood, it has undoubtedly an intercultural function which closely fits with Marks' definition of the intercultural:

> Intercultural indicates a context that cannot be confined to a single culture. It also suggests movement between one culture and another, thus implying diachrony and the possibility of transformation. It means that a work is not the property of a single culture but mediates in at least two directions. It accounts for the encounter between cultural cinema's synthesis of new forms of expression and new kinds of knowledge. (Marks 2000: 248)

The beggar's voice and song present a particularly complex layering of meanings, connotations and sonorities, and have a powerful corporeal effect on listeners' reception: an uncanny sense of disorientation, an alienating feeling of otherness and anxiety. A similar reaction is elicited by the scream of the vice consul in *India Song* and *Son nom de Venise dans Calcutta désert*, which we will now examine.

The vice consul's scream

The vice consul has a very special place in those films: in an act of madness, he shot at the lepers in Lahore and is now considered to be a social outcast by his colleagues. Invited by Anne-Marie Stretter to a reception held at the French Embassy, his arrival is accompanied by disparaging comments by guests. During a conversation with Anne-Marie Stretter at the party, he declares his love for her and says he is aware that other guests consider him to be mad. He says: 'Je parle faux/ma voix leur fait peur/de qui est-elle?' (I sound false/my voice scares them/whom does it come from?). It is the sound of his voice that scares the guests, anticipating what will happen to spectators when the vice consul screams.

In a major sequence lasting twenty-five minutes, including one shot of ten minutes, we hear the vice consul howling. The dissociation between the visual track and the soundtrack accentuates the intensity of the shout and its effects on the audience. On-screen, Michael Lonsdale, who is also the voice of the vice consul, stays mouth closed and stands immobile, inexpressive. In his autobiography the actor explains:

> I yelled my personal grief through this character. Sometimes an actor can heal himself through a role in a film, it can be liberating, and it is what happened. I was able to put all my grief into that scream and howl.[2] (Lonsdale 2016: 49)

If for Michael Lonsdale the experience was truly cathartic, for spectators this visceral scream will remain unforgettable, not through identification with the suffering of the visual character who shows no external sign of pain, but because of the physical and uncontrollable experience the sound triggers. As explained by Elliott, when a scream is heard, at first there is the initial and spontaneous reaction by the body and the ear. The sound can then be associated with various social and cultural codes, in this case psychological suffering and distress. Finally, the listener understands the reason of the scream through 'a form of corporeal mimesis and transitivism' (Elliott 2011: 148).

In *Les Lieux de Marguerite Duras*, the filmmaker explains the meaning of the vice consul's scream, which she links to the baby's first cry at birth:

> The first sign of life is a cry of pain … It is more than a cry, you know. It is the cry of someone who is being killed, whose throat is being slit, the cry of someone who does not want.[3] (Duras and Porte 1977: 23)

Several meanings have been given by Duras to the voice, but this time, the voice cuts across cultures and by referring to a biological situation: the primal scream, which emphasises the link with the maternal symbiosis. It is the characteristics of the howling voice – its loudness, its viscerality, as if coming from the depth of Lonsdale's body – and the duration of the scream that affect spectators and provoke powerful, bodily reactions: suspension of breath, shivering, skin crawling, tension in the throat and neck, and other strong physical reactions that affect them before they have time to think about what is actually taking place. The whole sequence of the vice consul's scream is an excruciating experience for most film viewers, which powerfully illustrates Sonnenschein's study on power of sound in film and its effects, on the body which we have already mentioned (Sonnenschein 2001: 71).

For Chion, 'Duras' films involve the sight of mute bodies and the sound of voices one could attribute to them, but always with a slippage, a space in-between' (Chion 1999: 100). However, it does not matter who the voice belongs to and that it is detached from the image of Michael Lonsdale on-screen, because the vice consul's howling is meaningful in itself, just because of its corporeal effects on spectators, who can experience the psychological pain of separation.

In the preceding chapters on the disjunction of sound and image and on the visual track, I explored the notion of nociception. The non-semantic vocalisations of the vice consul also conjure nociception through the intensity and the rawness of the voice, with its visceral impact on listeners, although there is no feeling of empathy towards the character, who is just an audio-visual construction. Nociception is clearly detached from the narrative and is triggered by auditory perception of pain. It is an experience of the senses, as already demonstrated in our study.

Silence

With the coming of sound film, not only was the expressive use of the voice released, but so was the use of silence. While silence is often understood as the absence of sound, or the absence of music, in Duras' films, this is not the case. Silence has an independent function regarding the narrative and contributes to the rhythm of the film. Silences and long pauses are often non-diegetic and basically semantically meaningless, but it is impossible not to notice or feel them as they sometimes last several minutes. It has already been shown that long pauses and silences fragment and threaten the logic of discourse as phrases are left hanging without any resolution or finality. Similarly, long silences between shots emphasise the natural fragmentation of the filmic medium, composed of independent shots artificially assembled.

Silences are essential to speech, as blank spaces are to writing: they are indispensable to the construction of meaning, but if they become excessive they start disturbing the logic of discourse. In *Woman to Woman*, Duras explains that 'blanks turn up, you see. It happens like this – I'll try to explain: perhaps the blanks appear as a result of a violent rejection of syntax. Yes, I think that's it: that sounds right' (Duras and Gauthier 1987: 1). The overuse of silence has been closely linked by Duras and Duras scholars to the destructive process inherent in the work of the author, similar to the black screen. However, Duras has also given silence a feminist interpretation when she writes: 'In ancient times, in the past, for thousands of years, silence is women'[4] (Duras 2014b: 364). She clearly suggests that silence is synonymous to women's oppression by the patriarchal order, but she also intimates in *Woman to Woman* that it is an important element for the expression of female subjectivity and for feminine writing. Gaps, voids, silences and pauses are understood as sites of female oppression. However, female filmmakers (such as Chantal Akerman) often insert long silences so they can be heard, and the silence of oppression is no longer 'silenced', which is clearly the case in *Nathalie Granger*. It may mean for women a way to regain agency, and to express feminine interiority and subjectivity. This has been commented on by Bolton: 'For Irigaray, silence is a gesture that is a necessary starting point for both interiority and dialogue. Silence is an opportunity for women to experience the world, themselves, and the other without dissipation' (Bolton 2011: 86).

Irigaray has raised the question of the expression of female oppression in the visual arts and emphasised the importance of inserting gaps, silences and pauses with the double purpose of making female oppression heard and disrupting the masculine logic of discourse. In *Woman to Woman*, Duras described the bodily experience of silence in speech and linked it to her writing process as a woman:

> I know that the place where this writes itself, where I write it – when I do – is a place where breathing is shortened and there is a drop in sensory perception. Not everything is heard, only certain things, you see. This is a black and white place. If there is colour, it gets added on. (Duras and Gauthier 1987: 2)

Silence can indeed be likened to a suspension of breath and a diminished sensory perception, and for spectators the extreme length of silences not justified by the narrative does produce a feeling of unease, perhaps even of suffocation, self-awareness and interiority. For Elliott, long silences have powerful effects, they provide a moment of pure sensory intensity: this pure sonic image 'acts upon the audience in a different way to the sensory motor linkage of movement-image ... It represents an escape from the world of clichés and ... provides a moment of pure sensory intensity' (Elliott 2011: 150).

In her analysis of silence in female film characters, Bolton suggests that silence in cinema

> might be used to challenge the visibility and accessibility of character and to complicate representation and reception. So, silence and pauses, as opposed to dialogue, could convey interiority without perhaps requiring obvious articulation or

representation: just as the spectator watches in silence, so they witness the woman on-screen experiencing self-reflection and repose. (Bolton 2011: 52)

Although in Duras' desynchronised films, actors on-screen are silent, silence on the soundtrack does not always belong to particular characters but is a device susceptible to make spectators experience 'self-reflection and repose', a breathing space outside of the film's diegesis. While silence can be given multiple meanings according to Duras and feminist scholars, for spectators it is first of all experienced by the senses, it is heard and felt, and as an embodied perception it can give them a lived experience of oppression and of internal reflection constituting the expression of women's subjectivities.

In our study of *Nathalie Granger*, we remarked on the suffocating atmosphere of the film indicative of the female characters' oppression, expressed through silence, and slow aural delivery and physical movements. Female characters in *Nathalie Granger* seem to be unable to breathe freely, a characteristic which can be extended to all the female protagonists in Duras' films and which contributes to spectators' embodied reactions. As Chion suggests, there is a connection between hearing and the viewer's own breathing: 'Breathing noises in a film can directly affect our own respiration' (Chion 1994: 34), as can the suspension of breath or its rarefaction.

Writing and the voice

Duras' experimentation with the voice in *Le Camion* is also relevant to our examination of the sonic experience, as the film sheds light on the links between the voice and feminine writing, *écrire femme*. This is particularly interesting because Duras (with Gérard Depardieu) reads the dialogues of the film, which allows us to link more closely the film to her own statement on writing and her female voice. In an interview about *Le Camion*, she explicitly associates writing and the voice: 'I read *The Lorry* as I hear writing take place. Before its projection on the page, one hears it. Before a sentence emerges, it is heard' (Duras 1987b: 102). Hélène Cixous called this '*la venue à l'écriture*' ('the coming to writing')

(Cixous 1991), a silent and ephemeral phase of the writing process, and a state of expectant inspiration. In *Le Camion*, Duras and Depardieu attempt to reproduce this initial phase of writing, this internal voice or as Duras called it '*la voix de la lecture intérieure*' ('the voice of internal reading') which is what 'I hear when I write' (Duras 1987b: 104). This phase is an archaic state of the writing process, as it is still bound to the body. Roland Barthes named it '*l'écriture à haute voix*' ('writing aloud'), explaining that:

> Its aim is not the clarity of the messages, the theatre of emotions: what it searches for (in a perspective of bliss) are the pulsional incidents, the language lined with flesh, a text where we can hear the grain of the throat, the patina of consonants, the voluptuousness of vowels, a whole carnal stereophony: the articulation of the body, of the tongue, not that of meaning, of language. (Barthes 1975: 66–7)

What Duras wants spectators to hear is not so much the meaning of the dialogues, which is often illogical and incoherent, but the rustling of the body, the presence of the flesh, the rattling of the air against the vocal cords. The voice in all of Duras' films points to the corporeity of writing and to the erotic stripping of meaning:

> This slowness, this lack of discipline in punctuating the text is as if I were undressing the words, one after another and I discover what was underneath, the isolated, unrecognisable word, stripped of any kinship, of any identity, abandoned. (Duras 1990: 71)

Like Duras, the French scholars Cixous, Irigaray and Kristeva have all linked the voice to the notion of *écriture féminine*:

> I sense femininity in writing by: a privilege of *voice: writing and voice* are intertwined and interwoven, and writing's continuity/ voice's rhythm take each other's breath away through interchanging, make the text gasp or form it out of suspenses and silences, make it lose its voice or rend it with cries. (Cixous and Clément 1986: 92)

Duras' experimentation with the voice in her films cannot be divorced from the feminist preoccupations of her time with *écriture féminine*.

However, it also has strong links with recent scholarship of embodied spectatorship because of its emphasis on non-semantic elements in cinema, including the materiality of the voice.

The more recent scholarly exploration of embodied spectatorship and intercultural cinema bears important similarities with the work of the 1970s' French feminist theorists. Although there is reluctance to link the conceptualisation of the haptic with the feminine, because of the threat of essentialism, even Marks admits that 'in a sexual positioning, that oscillates between mother- and father-identification, it seems that haptic visuality is on the side of the mother' (Marks 2000: 188). The following study of music will lead to similar conclusions.

Music

Duras often talked about her feelings toward music. She wrote: 'Music terrifies me ... moves me profoundly' (Duras 1977: 39). But music is also fundamental to her cinema and all her films include music, mostly non-diegetic. Like every other element of the soundtrack, its impact on spectators is powerful and it transgresses the role traditionally assigned to it. While non-diegetic music is supposed to stay in the background and is only there to clarify the narrative without being noticed, its place in Duras' films is on the contrary central and an integral part of the film structure. It also serves to destabilise, decentre and complicate the narrative (Everett 2000: 23).

India Song is famous for its soundtrack, not only for the use of the female voice but also for the music. It is structured around two powerful music compositions: the banal but catchy blues melody 'India Song', composed especially for the film by Carlos d'Alessio, and Beethoven's fourteenth Diabelli Variation. While 'India Song' evokes the place and period of the story, the1930s, its association with the dance performed by the actors on-screen provokes in spectators a kinaesthetic reaction, a desire to dance and to love. As rightly commented by the vice consul, 'this tune makes me want to love'; it is not surprising that it became a popular tune, a hit song (sang by Jeanne Moreau), and that it stayed in spectators' memories long after the screening of the film.

According to Everett, who focused her study on the role of music in Duras' films, the fourteenth Diabelli Variation

> whose contrapuntal relationship with 'India Song' lies at the heart of the film's structure, itself develops complex layers of introversion, memory and desire due to its association with the death and absence of the main character (Anne-Marie Stretter), as well as with (the memory of) her life, since she was a pianist for whom music had become unbearably painful. (Everett 2000: 24)

While Everett rightly links the music to the narrative and the characters, this intellectual approach takes the perspective of the projected sound rather than the way it is perceived and embodied by spectators. Music is not just sound; it is rhythmical pause and melodious movement which 'not only acts upon our sense organs, causing them to participate in it, but communicates itself to all our simultaneous impressions' (Kracauer 1960: 135). Music affects the body in its entirety, provoking strong emotions and affecting all senses including the sense of space and movement. When music is heard by the audience it goes straight to their sensorium and then linked to themes, narratives and characters.

Duras has used the same music in different films: for example, the Diabelli Variation is heard in *Des journées entières dans les arbres*, *India Song* and *Le Camion*, and is played by the child in *Moderato Cantabile*. For Duras' spectators, music triggers memories of past screenings and provokes a sense of familiarity, involving them directly and creatively in a similar way to the recycling of the visual sequences in *L'Homme atlantique* and the audio track in *Son nom de Venise dans Calcutta désert*. In *Nathalie Granger*, the seven notes of a Czerny study played over and over by Nathalie create a feeling of profound sadness and isolation, echoing the sense of loss experienced by Nathalie's mother.

Music has been associated by gender theorists to the feminine, like the female voice and silence. For Irigaray, it precedes linguistic codes and has a similar place in the acquisition of language as Kristeva' semiotic chora:

> In utero, I see nothing (except darkness?), but I hear. Music comes before meaning. A sort of preliminary to meaning, coming after warmth, moisture, softness, kinesthesis. Do I hear first of all? After

touch. But I cannot hear without touching; nor see, moreover. I hear, and what I hear is sexually differentiated. Voice is differentiated. (Irigaray 1993a: 140–1)

In *India Song*, there seems to exist an in-between space, neither diegetic nor non-diegetic, when the couple dancing on-screen intertwines with the music, to create a haptic moment when spectators' embodiment is strongly kinetic and takes them out of the film space into embodied feelings: a physical desire to dance and to move. 'India Song' is a piece of music that arouses emotional response; it establishes a moment which is outside the narrative in a special space. Music in Duras' films, including *Les Enfants*, always establishes moments of spectators' embodiment outside the narrative, either kinetic or emotional, sometimes, as in the case of *Les Enfants*, adding a humoristic perspective.

As such, music also offers an energy that can circulate as breath between inside and outside, a direct communication between the film and the body of its aural spectators. It penetrates the skin and resonates with the body of listeners, and, as suggested by Nancy, like 'a blow from the outside, clamor from within, this sonorous, sonorized body undertakes a simultaneous listening to a "self" and to a "world" that are both in resonance' (Nancy 2007: 43).

In *Aurélia Steiner (Melbourne)*, the engine of the boat has the role of music and in *Les Mains négatives*, the music on the violin which plays during the travelling shots is like a scraping sound that has an irritating effect on listeners. So, music in Duras' films is not always melodic, although she did use Beethoven's and Bach's piano music in many films. It can also take on the role of sound effects, blurring the distinction between music and noise.

Sound effects

Noise is an element of the sensory world that is totally devalued on the aesthetic level. It is often ignored by theorists and film scholars. According to Chion, sound effects are 'the repressed part of film not just in practice but also in analysis' (Chion 1994: 144). This can be explained by the fact that sound effects and natural noises have the function of reinforcing the presence of visible objects, so they, themselves, become invisible. Their primary function is a realistic one, aiming at contributing to the film's coherence and unity. In Duras' films this function is rarely used, but natural sounds such as water lapping, birds singing, dogs barking and so on, evoke a particular atmosphere and have an important role similar at times to that of music, because of their melody and their rhythmic reoccurrence. Natural sounds contribute effectively to the soundscape, although they are seldom synchronised with the image, nor is the source of the sound represented on-screen. Their role consists in providing breathing space and rhythm to the films, in constructing a geographical environment, and sometimes in evoking a complex political reality. Sound effects can produce a sense of proximity or distance, but in Duras' films they often disturb the spatial coherence of the film, and exterior sounds can invade interior spaces and vice versa. This interpenetration of interior and exterior has political meaning in *India Song*. It suggests a tense relationship between the inside of the embassy (the site of colonising powers) and the outside (colonised India), and has threatening connotations. It also disconcerts spectators' sense of space.

In *Nathalie Granger*, noises have been selected to reinforce the theme of the film, the role and condition of women. They are interior sounds (of a chair being moved, the clatter of dishes, a telephone ringing, doors shutting, people walking) and exterior noises (water lapping, fire crackling). They all reinforce the meanings of the film by stressing the activities of women in the house and in the garden. The difference between the sound of women and men moving is also stressed: women walk softly around the house, as lightly as the cat, whereas the salesman walks noisily through the house. Women and men act differently in the domestic space.

Aurélia Steiner (Melbourne) uses sound effects differently, as background music: the noise of the engine of the boat dominates the filmic space with no narrative justifications, the intensity of its roar varies, producing sonic zooms while the camera, obviously on a barge, films the river Seine. Although the sound of the engine is disconnected from the story being told, it is similar to background music: it is neither 'off' nor 'on', since it could come from one of the boats or even the barge. The film problematises the status of sound effects, not only when they are used as background music but also because they are never clearly inside or outside the frame. This exposes the material ambiguity and materiality of sound effects and is in accordance with Metz' analysis of the misconception of the status of sound. He explains that:

> In a film, a sound is considered 'off' (literally 'off screen') when in fact it is the sound's source that is off screen … We tend to forget that a sound is never 'off': either it is audible or it doesn't exist. When it exists, it could not possibly be situated within the interior of the rectangle or outside of it, since the nature of the sounds is to diffuse themselves more or less into the entire surrounding space: sound is simultaneously 'in' the screen, in front, behind, around, and throughout the entire movie theatre. (Metz 1980: 29)

The characteristics of a sound, including its intensity and sonic qualities, are experienced by listeners before the source of the sound is identified and the sound named. So, although, as we have mentioned, Duras' films use sounds as a political or gender device, they are heard before they are identified or interpreted as such. Sometimes their source cannot be clearly recognised and listeners, especially with *India Song*, may wonder whether they come from an animal or a human being. According to Elliott (2011: 155), sound effects are what they are: pure sound waves that travel through the air affecting audience members on several different corporeal levels. They are also connected to spectators' often unconscious memories. Studies on sound show that we are physically affected by the ways a film transmits sound and Elliott suggests that 'the ears of the skin provide us with the ground for an emotional response, not the other way around; it is this that represents the initial sensation out of which the emphatic and thus narratological elements are transformed' (Elliott 2011: 147).

Kristeva links sound to the time in childhood before language and society have taken on their full and fixed meanings for us. In her 1977 essay 'Stabat Mater' (Moil 1986), she evokes a sensual world in which the foetus, and subsequently the infant, and the mother are connected by sound without stable meaning: she points to the heartbeat and other bodily sounds carried by amniotic fluid, and to the lulling, cooing, burbling, gurgling sounds exchanged by mother and infant after birth. She calls this sound-world 'chora', meaning space/place, that which locates and contains us. As we have already mentioned, the semiotic chora is 'a rhythmic pulsion' rather than a new language. It constitutes the heterogeneous, disruptive dimension of language, that which can never be caught up in the limits of traditional linguistic theory.

Sound effects also create an intercultural dimension in the Indian cycle films, as they reconstitute a soundscape which, intertwined with long silences and with voices, resonate throughout the film as a foreign space.

Cinema allowed Duras to explore poetic language in its primary state as sounds, voice, howling, laughs, silence and music. With regard to perception, Chion (1994) asserts that sound can do more than the visual and that spectators' audition subconsciously structures their perception of the film. Duras carried the perceptive role of sound much further, by making spectators dependant on the auditory track to attempt to make sense of the film, because of the absence of synchronisation. However, the films do not satisfy the listeners' desire to make sense of the plot, but sound offers them the opportunity to sense it and be affected by it. Asked about the effect of the voice on spectators of film, Chion replied that:

> The cinema returns us to an infantile situation. Infants have no control over their body, they cannot get out of their bed. So, they are stuck, but they can see and hear, and so there is a very high level of perception. And the cinema brings us back to that situation … for children, in the earliest stages of infancy, the world really is that strange. They can hear voices, but they can't turn around so easily to see where the voices are coming from. The source of the voice is hidden … It's disturbing, terrifying, and sometimes even magical. I think the cinema gives us a link with something of this nature, something inside us, which has always been a part of us. (Chion 2017)

Chion seems to agree with gender theorists as he connects the effect of sounds, human and non-human, in cinema, with regression to early childhood. Duras, Kristeva and Irigaray relate hearing a poetic voice, unstructured sounds, silence and the emotionally and physically troubling effect these sounds have on spectators to an even earlier childhood and to the time before language and society have taken on their full and fixed meanings for us.

Murch begins his introduction to Chion's *Audio-Vision* by saying:

> We begin to hear before we are born, four and a half months
> after conception … From then on we develop in a continuous
> luxurious bath of sounds: the sound of our mother's voice, the
> swash of her breathing, the trumpeting of her intestines, the
> timpani of her heart […] Sound rules as solitary queen of our
> senses. (Murch in Chion 1994: VII)

In this chapter I have examined not only how sound can be interpreted
but also how it can be experienced by spectators as a form of knowledge
that extends beyond cognition and understanding. It is embodied
sensorial knowledge that is experiential rather than intellectual, at least
initially when auditory spectators are faced with the film. It can be linked
to the feminist theories of philosophers such as Irigaray, Kristeva and
Cixous on the feminine. Interestingly, we have shown complementary
perspectives in the work of sound specialists Chion and Sonnenschein
and of French feminist theorists. For all these thinkers, sound can have a
primary effect on the body unmediated by any sense of subjective identification; spectators' bodies react to certain kinds of music 'not only
because we are made scared, nervous, or anxious through generic codes
but through processes of biological and neurological reception' (Elliott
2011: 146). The ears provide us with the ground for an emotional
response, not the other way around; it is sound that represents the initial
sensation out of which the empathetic and thus narratological elements
are formed (Elliott 2011: 147).

The importance of the soundtracks in Duras' films reaffirms the
perspective we have developed throughout this study, that is, that the
powerful effects of the films are due to their extreme sensoriality, their
links to Duras' multisensorial female world and their connections with
spectators' sensoria.

Notes

1   (My translation) 'Au sommet, la parole, apte par sa richesse sémantique et
    structurale, à rivaliser avec l'image. Au centre, le bruit, destiné à obéir aux
    instructions de la diégèse représentée par l'image. Tout en bas, la musique, simple
    modulateur d'ambiance.'

2   (My translation) 'J'ai hurlé mon chagrin personnel à travers ce personage. Il arrive qu'on se soigne à travers un rôle, qu'on se libère, et c'est comme ça que je me suis donné et que j'ai pu investir dans des cris et des hurlements tout le chagrin que je vivais.'

3   (My translation) Le premier signe de vie est un hurlement de douleur . . . Plus qu'un cri, vous savez. C'est des cris d'égorgés, des cris de quelqu'un qu'on tue, qu'on assassine. Les cris de quelqu'un qui ne veut pas.'

4   (My translation) 'Dans les temps anciens, dans les temps reculés, depuis des millénaires, le silence, c'est les femmes.'

Conclusion

This book has attempted to reveal the connections between the innovative formal strategies employed by Duras in her films, female subjectivity and the feminine, and the multiple layers of spectatorial embodiment. Film theories and criticism have tended to exclude the sensory body from analysis, and this has particularly been the case with films perceived as difficult or intellectual like those of Duras. This has had the effect of obliterating a whole area of investigation, limiting the studies of Duras' films to textual analyses and excluding the viewers' reactions to her films from the realm of analysis.

The ability of Duras' films to provoke aesthetic reactions and feelings of excitement, wonder, languor, desire, but also anxiety, oppression, alienation, loss and lack has always been recognised, however, if not analysed. The lack of interest in embodied spectatorship in Duras' films by scholars can also be linked in many instances to the silencing of the forms of expression of the feminine in mainstream cinema, theory and criticism. My approach to the films which integrates phenomenological, neuroscientific, embodiment and feminist theories provides new alternatives to the study of Duras' work and a new understanding of her films. It has allowed me to show that sounds and images trigger viewers' and listeners' embodied reactions, sensorial synaesthetic experiences, while responses such as nociception, thermoception, tactility and olfaction, as well as those related to vestibular and kinaesthetic systems can also arise as a result of Duras' use of the audio-visual medium. The sensory experiences are all imbricated and this multisensoriality cannot be divorced from Duras' female experience, in our analysis. Elliott's *Hitchcock and the Cinema of Sensations*, while devoting a very useful theoretical chapter to gender theories and their links to multisensoriality, does not integrate sexual difference in his analyses of Hitchcock's films, assuming a gender-neutral perspective and consequently running the risk of reproducing the hidden power relations intrinsic to mainstream cinema and film theory.

Duras' films are innovatory and create new forms of filmic expressions as well as new experiences for spectators by changing our perception and embodied reception of visual and sonic elements. Hence, I have focused on the medium rather than on the representation of female characters to study female subjectivity and the feminine. The attempts made throughout the book to outline a feminine cinematics, to use Bainbridge's (2008) terminology, depend therefore on paying close attention to the materiality of the medium: the image, the sound and the relationships between them.

The concept of multisensoriality has led me to bring together many elements. First of all, Duras' interculturality was shown to be perceived through the insertion of haptic memories, what Marks called 'cultural sensoria' (2000: 243) – visual, sonic, olfactic or thermic – often in very subtle ways, as Duras never filmed scenes happening in the places of her childhood, such as Vietnam or Cambodia. The shimmering red dress in *Le Navire Night*, the beggar's voice, the burning incense and the music in *India Song*, the sound of the engine of a barge in *Aurélia Steiner (Melbourne)*, the tropical heat and the wintery cold of *Agatha*, recurrent shots of the sea, are all indicative of the process of the subtle return of childhood memories, confirming that 'a memory is precious in inverse proportion to its ability to be externalized and expressed' (Marks 2000: 243). What is the most valuable for an understanding of intercultural artists, according to Marks, is to think of the film 'not as a screen, but as a membrane, that brings its audience into contact with the material forms of memory' (Marks 2000: 243). As we have shown, the notion of membrane is, however, not only visual in Duras' films but also auditory, a tympanic membrane turning viewers into 'acoustic spectators', to use Fox's (2017) expression.

Secondly, the female viewpoint was found to result from Duras' innovative approach to the medium and the synaesthetic and multimodal reaction of spectators to the films. The primacy of sonic elements, the rhythm of the films, the abundance of tactile shots were linked to French feminist theories on the feminine, and we have been able to show that Duras' formal innovations represent a subversion of the power relations at work in mainstream cinema and an attempt at bringing the oppressed elements of film linked to the feminine to the fore.

Thirdly, sound has been given a central place in this study, although theoretical work in this area is not as developed as is the case with synaesthetic and haptic studies of the visual track. However, we were able to intersect Chion's concept of audio-vision, Shaeffer's acoustics studies and Irigaray's theories to reveal – through the analyses of the films – a geography of sounds linked to intercultural memories and the feminine.

Finally, my approach to the study of the visual track shows that Duras' images provide spectators, male or female, with a new way of considering films, which in turn leads to a new understanding of the role and effects of images in Duras' work. To uncover layers of under-standing of spectactorial engagement that may ordinarily have remained unnoticed extends our appreciation of the filmic work of Duras as well as the relationships her images have with viewers. Sensual knowledge is vital to our grasp of the power of Duras' films. As she herself declared, 'I am not yet up to what I have found in cinema. I will be dead when one finds why it is so powerful[1] (Duras 2014b: 937), suggesting not only that our understanding of cinema and its impact on audiences would evolve towards a better comprehension of the effects of her films on spectators, but also that her cinema was visionary.

Embodied film theory, French feminist theories, neuroscience and phenomenological approaches are often criticised for negating the political dimension of films, and cultural and racial differences. However, I have emphasised throughout the book that Duras' engagement in cinema is fundamentally political, subversive of power relations, aware of gender, racial and cultural differences and that it is precisely because of this profound questioning of dominant cinema and repre-sentational strategies that a multifaceted approach that does not focus on narrative analysis is necessary. Once the films are peeled away from their conventions, their materiality is exposed and the effect on viewers becomes an intriguing area of investigation. By using the work of Marks on intercultural cinema, Elliott on embodied spectatorship, Antunes on the multisensory perception of film, Quinlivan on breath in cinema, Irigaray on gender theory, and innovative studies of films and female subjectivity by Bolton and Bainbridge, I have been able to reveal the close imbrications of Duras' subjectivity, subversive power and formal film strategies, and their effect on viewers and listeners.

In this book, I have in some ways assumed that all spectators would respond similarly to Duras' films. Of course, this is never the case, as some viewers find the films boring, others, intellectually stimulating but not particularly physically engaging. Similarly, our feminist reading of her cinema may seem to imply that all female authors, filmmakers and spectators would act and react in a similar fashion. This is indeed a difficulty with these types of analyses, but as observed by Elliott, 'it is no different . . . from supposing everyone's experience of sexuality is similar, that claustrophobia is always a disturbing experience or that all viewers do not want to be killed in the shower by Tony Perkins' (Elliott 2011: 185). Whenever possible, however, we have mentioned possible reactions from spectators from non-European cultures, especially in our analysis of *India song*. This study does not pretend to cover all aspects and characteristics of spectatorship of Duras' films, but it is hoped that it will mark the beginning of a new direction in Durassian studies that focus on viewers' reception rather than solely on films as texts, and take into account French feminist theories on female subjectivity.

If Duras' films refract, as I have shown, the gender and cinematographic debates of their time, her work has also had a lasting impact on authors, filmmakers and visual artists, beyond the twentieth century. Claire Denis, for example, has clearly claimed filiation with Duras and her films (Adler 2013). In a radio interview for the hundredth anniversary of Duras' birth, she said she felt close to Duras' hybrid identity, her interculturality, colonial childhood and feeling of exile in France. Scholarly studies such as McMahon (2008) have shown a sensorial approach to Denis' films with connections with our own methodology. Other female filmmakers such as Chantal Ackerman and Sally Potter, although not always in full agreement with Duras' approach to films, have recognised her influence.

For the hundredth anniversary of Duras' birth, in 2014, the Pompidou Centre in Paris organised an exhibition entitled 'Duras Song' curated by visual and artistic director Thu Van Tran and art critic Jean-Max Colars. For the occasion, a full retrospective of her filmography was screened. The exhibition turned the life and work of Duras, including her writing process, into a work of art which assembled manuscripts, typescripts, newspaper articles, photos, audio-visual material, fiction films and documentaries. It was a resolutely contemporary experience as it took visitors on a journey punctuated with light tables that turned on and off as they walked past while projected film clips demonstrated Duras' relevance for visual artists. The exhibition also showed the timelessness of Duras' literary, theatrical and filmic engagement which is confirmed by the number of her plays being performed on stage every year in France and overseas and the new film based on *La Douleur* (2017, *Memoir of Pain*) by Emmanuel Finkiel with actors Mélanie Thierry and Benoît Magimel. In the new productions, whether literary or film adaptations, Duras' film innovations such as the primacy given to the voice-over, to the music and silence, as well as a bare visual aesthetic, are always fundamental to these new works.

Duras' literature and cinema inspired poets, writers, musicians, actors, singers, filmmakers and photographers from diverse cultures, and they continue to engender new artistic, literary, theatrical and cinematic creations in France and across the world. The exhibition was symptomatic of this momentum and revealed that Duras was a unique and visionary author and filmmaker, who reinvented the relationship between narrative, image, sound and viewer. Her films have remained captivating, disconcerting and poetic for young audiences and are still able to anticipate and pave the way for twentieth-first-century visual artists.

The impact of Duras' films is not always straightforward, but similarities, links and associations can be seen between some contemporary artists' and filmmakers' work and the films and texts of Duras. Contemporary visual artist, Vietnamese-born Thu Van Tran, based some of her work on Duras' texts and films to produce several pieces of great interest, including a personal translation of Joseph Conrad's colonial-era novel *Heart of Darkness*, several sculptures and installations such as 'Le nombre pur' and 'La bibliothèque des ouvriers' based on Duras' texts, and, more recently, short super 8mm films, available on Tran's website. Duras' influence is also obvious in the treatment of the theme of Vietnam, the political references and the style of the films, with the abundance of haptic close-ups emphasising tactile and sensorial experiences.

If Duras' films and novels have shaken and inspired the literary, cinema and art scene in France in the twentieth and twenty-first centuries, the ripples can also be felt throughout the world and would be worthy of scholarly investigation. The influence of Duras' films on contemporary artists is pervasive, as can be seen in the work of video artists such as Alejandro Cesarco (Uruguay), Cao Fei (China), Jimmy

Robert (Belgium), and Banthum Ratmanee and Wasarut Unaprom to cite a few,[2] but the studies of their work remain sporadic.

The legacy of Duras' cinema is an area that would require further exploration, not only in the French-speaking and anglophone world but also in the Latin American and Asian contexts where Duras' writing has had a recognised influence. *The Lover* (1984) was published in twenty-nine languages, including three in separate Chinese dialects, according to publisher Jérôme Lindon (Garis 1991), so the influence of Duras' work on filmmakers and writers in the world is currently difficult to assess and would require intercultural and multilingual research.

Notes

1   (My translation) 'Je ne suis pas encore à la hauteur de ce que j'ai trouvé au cinéma. Je serai morte quand on aura trouvé pourquoi c'est tellement fort.'

2   The work of Cesarco, Fei and Robert led to interesting analyses from Dominique Villeneuve in his paper '"Tu me tues, tu me fais du bien" ou une résonance de l'œuvre de Marguerite Duras dans les œuvres de vidéastes du 21ème siècle' at the conference 'Duras and the Arts', held in Sydney in July 2016. Thai artists Ratmanee and Unaprom presented their work on Duras, in a paper titled 'De l'ivresse du texte à la représentation théâtrale dans "An Epilogue to *The Malady of Death*"' at the above-mentioned conference.

Bibliography

Adler, Laure (2001), *Marguerite Duras: a Life*, translated by Anne-Marie Glasheen, London: Phoenix.

—— (2013), 'Duras passionnément 3/5', *Hors-Champs*, France Culture, 3 April, <https://www.franceculture.fr/emissions/hors-champs/marguerite-duras-passionnement-35> (last accessed 1 February 2018).

Antunes, Luis R. (2016), *The Multisensory Film Experience: a Cognitive Model of Experiential Film Aesthetics*, Bristol, Chicago: Intellect. ebook.

Anzieu, Didier (1981), *Le corps de l'œuvre: essais psychanalytiques sur le travail créateur*, Paris: Gallimard.

—— (1995), *Le Moi peau*, Paris: Dunod.

Bainbridge, Caroline (2008), *A Feminine Cinematics: Luce Irigaray, Women and Film*, Basingstoke, New York: Palgrave Macmillan.

Barker, Jennifer (2009), *The Tactile Eye: Touch and the Cinematic Experience*, Berkeley: University of California Press.

Barthes, Roland (1975), *The Pleasure of the Text*, translated by Richard Miller, New York: Hill and Wang.

—— (1997), 'The Grain of the Voice', translated by Stephen Heath in *Image, Music, Text*, London: Fontana, pp. 179–89.

Baudry, Jean-Louis and Alan Williams, (1974), 'Ideological Effects of the Basic Cinematographic Apparatus', *Film Quarterly*, 28: 2 (Winter, 1974–5), pp. 39–47.

Beauvoir, Simone de (2010), *The Second Sex*, translated by Constance Borde and Sheila Malovany-Chevallier, New York: Alfred A. Knopf.

Bénos, Rémi and Samuel Challéat (2014), '"Outrenuit": penser les ressources environnementales nocturnes avec Pierre Soulages', *Carnets du Collectif RENOIR – Ressources Environnementales Nocturnes*, 30 July, <https://renoir.hypotheses.org/655> (last accessed 5 January 2017).

Betton, Gérard (1983), *Esthétique du cinéma*, Paris: P.U.F.

Beugnet, Martine (2007, 2012), *Cinema and Sensation: French Cinema and the Art of Transgression*, Edinburgh: Edinburgh University Press.

—— (2008), 'Cinema and Sensation: Contemporary French Film and Cinematic Corporeality', *Paragraph*, 31: 2 (July), pp. 173–88.

Bolton, Lucy (2011), *Film and Female Consciousness: Irigaray, Cinema and Thinking Women*, London: Palgrave Macmillan.

Borgomano, Madeleine (2009), 'The Image of the Cinema in *The Sea Wall*', in Rosanna Maule and Julie Beaulieu (eds), *In the Dark Room: Marguerite Duras and Cinema*, Oxford, Bern, Berlin: Peter Lang, pp. 65–86.

Bordwell, David (1997), *On the History of Film Style*, Cambridge, MA: Harvard University Press.

Brinkema, Eugenie (2014), *The Forms of the Affects*, Durham, NC: Duke University Press.

Burke, Carolyn, Naomi Schor and Margaret Whitford (eds) (1994), *Engaging With Luce Irigaray*, New York: Columbia University Press.

Butler, Alison (2002), *Women's Cinema: the Contested Screen*, London, New York: Wallflower.

Chamarette, Jenny (2015), 'Embodied Worlds and Situated Bodies: Feminism, Phenomenology, Film Theory', *Signs*, 40: 2, pp. 289–95Chateau, Dominique (1976), 'Pour une sémiologie des relations audio-visuelles dans le film', *Musique en jeu*, 23, April.

Chion, Michel (1985), *Le son au cinéma*, Paris: Cahiers du Cinéma/Éditions de l'étoile.

—— (1994), *Audio-Vision: Sound on Screen*, translated by Claudia Gorbman, New York: Columbia University Press.

—— (1999), *The Voice in Cinema*, translated by Claudia Gorbman, New York: Columbia University Press.

—— (2017), 'The Audio-Spectator: an Interview with Michel Chion', *Senses of Cinema*, September 2017, <http://sensesofcinema.com/2017/feature-articles/audio-spectator-interview-michel-chion/> (last accessed 8 October 2017).

Cixous, Hélène (1991), *'Coming to Writing' and Other Essays*, Cambridge, MA: Harvard University Press.

Cixous, Hélène and Catherine Clément (1986), *The Newly Born Woman*, Minneapolis: University of Minneapolis Press.

Coulthard, Lisa (2012), 'Haptic Aurality: Listening to the Films of Michael Haneke', *Film- Philosophy*, 16:1, pp. 16–29.

Cousseau, Anne (2002), 'Aventures poétiques' in B. Alazet, C. Blot-Labarrère, R. Harvey (eds), *Marguerite Duras, la tentation poétique*, Paris: Presses Sorbonne Nouvelle.

Cytowic, Richard (2002), *Synaesthesia: a Union of the Senses*, Cambridge, MA: MIT Press.

Deleuze, Gilles (1989), *Cinema 2: the Time-Image*, translated by Hugh Tomlinson and Robert Galeta, London: The Athlone Press.

—— (1992), *Cinema 1: the Movement-Image*, translated by Hugh Tomlinson and Barbara Habberjam, London: The Athlone Press.

—— (2003), *Francis Bacon: the Logic of Sensation*, London: Continuum.

Duras, Marguerite (1950), *Un barrage contre le Pacifique*, Paris: Gallimard.

—— (1977), *Le Camion suivi de l'entretien avec Michelle Porte*, Paris: Minuit.

—— (1981), 'Le Noir atlantique', *Des femmes en mouvement*, 57, 11–18 September, p. 30.

—— (1986), 'Duras toute entière', interview by Pierre Bénichou and Hervé Le Masson, *Le Nouvel Observateur*, 14–19 November, p. 57.

—— (1987a), *La Vie matérielle*, Paris: POL.

—— (1987b), *Marguerite Duras*, translated by Edith Cohen and Peter Connor, San Francisco: City Lights Books.

—— (1990), *Green Eyes*, translated by Carol Barko, New York: Columbia University Press.

—— (1991), *L'Amant de la Chine du Nord*, Paris: Gallimard.

—— (2006), *The Lover*, translated by Barbara Bray, London: Harper Perennial. Kindle version.

—— (2011a), *Œuvres complètes*, sous la direction de Gilles Philippe, I, Paris: Gallimard, Collection Bibliothèque de la Pléiade.

—— (2011b), *Œuvres complètes*, sous la direction de Gilles Philippe, II, Paris: Gallimard, Collection Bibliothèque de la Pléiade.

—— (2014a), *Œuvres complètes*, sous la direction de Gilles Philippe, III, Paris: Gallimard, Collection Bibliothèque de la Pléiade.

—— (2014b), *Œuvres complètes*, sous la direction de Gilles Philippe, IV, Paris: Gallimard, Collection Bibliothèque de la Pléiade.

—— (2014c), *Le Livre dit. Entretiens de Duras filme*, Paris: Gallimard.

Duras, Marguerite and Michelle Porte (1977), *Les Lieux de Marguerite Duras*, Paris: Minuit.

Duras, Marguerite, Jacques Lacan, Maurice Blanchot, Dyonis Mascolo, Xavière Gauthier and Pierre Fedida (1979), *Marguerite Duras*, Paris: Albatros.

Duras, Marguerite and Xavière Gauthier (1987), *Woman to Woman*, Lincoln, NE, London: University of Nebraska Press.

Eisenstein, Sergei (1986), *The Film Sense*, edited and translated by Jay Leyda, London: Faber and Faber.

Elliott, Paul (2010), 'The Eye, The Brain, The Screen', *Excursions*, 1: 1 (June), pp. 1–16, <http://www.excursions-journal.org.uk/index.php/excursions/article/view/2> (last accessed 10 January 2018).

—— (2011), *Hitchcock and the Cinema of Sensations*, London: I. B. Tauris.

Elsaesser, Thomas (2003), '"Where were you, when"... or "I phone, therefore I am"', *PMLA*, Vol. 118, No. 1, pp. 120–2.

Everett, Wendy (2000), 'An Art of Fugue? The Polyphonic Cinema of Marguerite Duras', in James S. Williams (ed.), *Revisionning Duras: Film, Race and Sex*, Liverpool: Liverpool University Press, pp. 21–36.

Flanagan, Matthew (2008), 'Towards an Aesthetic of Slow in Contemporary Cinema' in *16:9, 6:29*, <http://www.16-9.dk/2008-11/side11_inenglish.htm> (last accessed 30 September 2017).

Fox, Albertine (2017), *Godard and Sound*, London: I. B. Tauris. ebook.

Gallese, Vittorio (2017a), 'Mirroring, a Liberated Embodied Simulation and Aesthetic Experience', in *Mirror Images. Reflections in Art and Medecine*, Kunstmuseum Thun: Verlag für moderne Kunst, pp. 27–37.

—— (2017b), 'Visions of the Body: Embodied Simulation and Aesthetic Experience', <https://humanitiesfutures.org/papers/visions-body-embodied-simulation-aesthetic-experience>, pp. 1–27 (last accessed May 2017).

Gallese, Vittorio and Michele Guerra (2012a), "From Mirror Neurons to Embodied Simulation", Part 1, <https://www.youtube.com/watch?v=PlV7F3MHuEk> (last accessed 28 January 2017).

—— (2012b) "From Mirror Neurons to Embodied Simulation", Part 2, <https://www.youtube.com/watch?v=COKWZjCd_rM> (last accessed 28 January 2017).

—— (2014), 'The Feeling of Motion: Camera Movements and Motor Cognition', *Cinéma & Cie*, XIV: 22/23, Spring/Fall, pp. 103–12.

Garis, Leslie (1991), 'The Life and Loves of Marguerite Duras', *The NY Times*, 20 October, <http://www.nytimes.com/1991/10/20/magazine/the-life-and-loves-of-marguerite-duras.html?pagewanted=all> (last accessed 1 February 2018).

Garwood, Ian and Liz Greene (2016), 'Breath and the Body of the Voice in Cinema', *Music, Sound, and The Moving Image*, 10: 2, Autumn, pp. 105–7.

Gordon, Kristyn (2008), 'Desire, Duras, and Melancholia: Theorizing Desire after the 'Affective Turn', *Feminist Review*, 89, pp. 16–33.

Grodal, Torben (2009), *Embodied Visions: Evolution, Emotion, Culture, and Film*, Oxford: Oxford University Press.

Günther, Renate (2002), *Marguerite Duras*, Manchester: Manchester University Press.

Hasson, Uri, Ohad Landesman, Barbara Knappmeyer, Ignacio Vallines, Nava Rubin and David J. Heeger (2008), 'Neurocinematics: the Neuroscience of Film', *Projections*, 2: 1, pp. 1–26, <http://www.cns.nyu.edu/~nava/MyPubs/Hasson-etal_Neuro-Cinematics2008.pdf> (last accessed 10 January 2018).

Hayward, Susan (1993), *French National Cinema*, London, New York: Routledge.

Heinrich, Nathalie (1980), 'Aurélia Steiner', *Cahiers du Cinéma*, 307, pp. 45–7.

Heyman, Stephen (2014), 'Pierre Soulages: Master of Black, Still Going Strong' 20 May, <https://www.nytimes.com/2014/05/21/arts/international/pierre-soulages-master-of-black-still-going-strong.html?_r=0> (last accessed 30 September 2017).

Hill, Leslie (1993), *Marguerite Duras: Apocalyptic Desires*, London, New York: Routledge.

Hole, Kristin (2016), *Towards a Feminist Cinematic Ethics: Claire Denis, Emmanuel Levinas and Jean-Luc Nancy*, Edinburgh: Edinburgh University Press.

Ince, Kate (2017), *The Body and the Screen: Female Subjectivity in Contemporary Women's Cinema*, New York, London: Bloomsbury.

Irigaray, Luce (1985a), *Speculum of the Other Woman*, translated by Gillian C. Gill, Ithaca: Cornell University Press.

—— (1985b), *This Sex Which Is Not One,* translated by Catherine Porter, Ithaca: Cornell University Press.

—— (1993a), *An Ethics of Sexual Difference,* translated by Carolyn Burke and Gillian C. Gill, Ithaca: Cornell University Press.

—— (1993b), *Je, tu, nous: Toward a Culture of Difference,* translated by Alison Martin, London, New York: Routledge.

—— (1996), *I Love to You: Sketch for a Possible Felicity in History,* translated by Alison Martin, London, New York: Routledge.

—— (1999), *The Forgetting of Air in Martin Heidegger,* translated by Mary Beth Mader, Austin: University of Texas.

—— (2002), *Dialogues,* a special issue of *Paragraph,* 25: 3, Edinburgh: Edinburgh University Press.

—— (2004a), *Key Writings:* London, New York: Continuum.

—— (2004b), 'The Age of the Breath' in *Key Writings:* London, New York: Continuum, pp. 165–70.

Kennedy, Barbara (2000), *Deleuze and Cinema: the Aesthetics of Sensation,* Edinburgh: Edinburgh University Press.

Kirshtner, Kelly (2005), 'Syn(aes)thesis: a Conversation of the Senses' *Octopus. A Journal of Visual Studies,* 1 (Fall), pp. 3–8.

Kracauer Siegfried (1960), *Theory of Film: the Redemption of Physical Reality,* Princeton: Princeton University Press.

Kristeva, Julia (1974), *La Révolution Du Langage Poétique: L'avant-Garde À La Fin Du XIXème Siècle, Lautréamont Et Mallarmé,* Paris: Seuil (abridged English translation: *Revolution in Poetic Language,* translated by Margaret Waller, New York: Columbia University Press, 1984.)

—— (1984), *Revolution in Poetic Language,* New York: Columbia University Press.

Lacan, Jacques (2001), 'Hommage à Marguerite Duras', in *Autres écrits,* Paris: Seuil, pp. 191–7.

Laine Tarja (2017), *Bodies in Pain: Emotion and the Cinema of Darren Aronofsky,* Oxford: Berghahn Books.

Laine, Tarja and Wanda Strauven (2009), 'The Synaesthetic Turn', *New Review of Film and Television Studies,* 7: 3, pp. 249–55.

Lebelley, Frédérique (1994), *Duras ou le poids d'une plume,* Paris: Grasset.

Lonsdale, Michael (2016), *Le Dictionnaire de ma vie,* Paris: Kero.

Marini, Marcelle (1977), *Territoires du féminin avec Marguerite Duras,* Paris: Minuit.

Marks, Laura U. (2000), *The Skin of the Film: Intercultural Cinema, Embodiment, and the Senses,* Durham, NC, London: Duke University Press. ebook.

—— (2002), *Touch: Sensuous Theory and Multisensory Media,* Minneapolis: University of Minnesota Press.

Martin, Angela (2008), 'Refocusing Authorship in Women's Filmmaking', in Barry Keith Grant (ed.), *Auteurs and Authorship: a Film Reader,* Malden, Oxford, Victoria: Blackwell Publishing, pp. 127–34.

Martin, Christian (2013), 'Bodies Without Limits in *Hiroshima mon amour*', *French Forum*, 38: 1–2, pp. 267–82.

Maule, Rosanna and Julie Beaulieu (eds) (2009), *In the Dark Room: Marguerite Duras and Cinema*, Oxford, Bern, Berlin: Peter Lang.

McFadden, Cybelle. (2016), *Gendered Frames, Embodied Camera: Varda, Akerman, Cabrera, Calle, and Maïwen*, Lanham, MD: Fairleigh Dickinson University Press.

McMahon, Laura (2008), 'Lovers in Touch: Inoperative Community in Nancy, Duras and *India Song*', *Paragraph*, 31: 2, pp. 189–205.

—— (2012), *Cinema and Contact: the Withdrawal of Touch in Nancy, Bresson, Duras and Denis*, London: Legenda.

Metz, Christian (1977), *Essais sémiotiques*, Paris: Klincksieck.

—— (1980), 'Aural Objects', *Yale French Studies*, 60, pp. 24–32.

Michaud, Jean and Raymond Bellour (1961), 'Agnès Varda de A à Z', *Cinéma 61*: 60, pp. 3–20.

Moil, Toril (1986), *The Kristeva Reader*, New York: Columbia University Press, <https://archive.org/stream/TheKristevaReader/The%20Kristeva%20Reader_djvu.txt> (last accessed 10 August 2017).

Mulvey, Laura (1975), 'Visual Pleasure and Narrative Cinema', *Screen*, 16: 3, pp. 6–18.

Murphy, Carol (2002), 'Reassessing Marguerite Duras', *Studies in 20th Century Literature*, 26: 1, pp. 1–15.

Nacache, Jacqueline (2012), 'The Actor as Icon of Presence: the Example of Delphine Seyrig', in Jörg Sternagel, Deborah Levitt, Dieter Mersch (eds), *Acting and Performance in Moving Image Culture: Bodies, Screens, Renderings*, Bielefeld: Verlag, pp. 159–76.

Nancy, Jean-Luc (2007), *Listening*, New York: Fordham University Press.

Noguez, Dominique (1984), *Edition vidéocritique des films de Marguerite Duras*, Paris: Ministère des Relations Extérieures.

Papendurg, Bettina and Marta Zazycka (eds) (2013), *Carn al Aesthetics: Transgressive Imaginary and Feminist Politics*, London: I. B. Tauris.

Powrie, Phil (2008), 'The Haptic Moment: Sparring with Paolo Conte in Ozon's *5x2*', *Paragraph: a Journal of Modern Critical Theory*, 31: 2, pp. 206–22.

Powell, Anna (2006), *Deleuze and Horror Films*, Edinburgh: Edinburgh University Press.

Pudovkin, Vsevolod, Sergei Eisenstein and Grigori Alexandrov (1985), 'A Statement', in Elisabeth Weis and John Belton (eds), *Film Sound: Theory and Practice*, New York: Columbia University Press, pp. 83–5.

Quinlivan, Davina (2012), *The Place of Breath in Cinema*, Edinburgh: Edinburgh University Press.

Ramanathan, Geetha (2006), *Feminist Auteurs: Reading Women's Films*, London, New York: Wallflower Press.

Resnais, Alain (1966), 'Propos d'Alain Resnais sur le cinéma', *L'Avant-scène du cinéma*, 61–2, pp. 48–51.

Rizzolatti, Giacomo and Lailia Craighero (2004), 'The Mirror Neuron System', in *Annual Review of Neuroscience*, 27, pp. 169–92.

Royer, Michelle (1990), 'Deconstruction of Masculinity and Femininity in the Films of Marguerite Duras', in Terry Threadgold and Anne Cranny-Francis (eds), *Feminine, Masculine and Representation*, Sydney, London, Boston, Wellington: Allen & Unwin, pp. 128–39.

—— (1997), *L'Écran de la passion: une étude du cinéma de Marguerite Duras*, Brisbane: Boombana Publications.

—— (2009), 'Writing, the Writing Self and the Cinema of Marguerite Duras', in Rosanna Maule and Julie Beaulieu (eds), *In the Dark Room: Marguerite Duras and Cinema*, Oxford, Bern, Berlin: Peter Lang, pp. 151–71.

—— (2014), 'Figures de l'hybridation dans les films de Marguerite Duras', in Florence de Chalonge, Yann Mével and Akido Ueda (eds), *Orients de Marguerite Duras*, Amsterdam, New York: Rodopi, pp. 191–203.

Russel-Watts, Linsey (2009), 'Analysing Sound and Voice: Refiguring Approaches to the Films of the "Indian Cycle"', in Rosanna Maule and Julie Beaulieu (eds), *In the Dark Room: Marguerite Duras and Cinema*, Oxford, Bern, Berlin: Peter Lang, pp. 235–55.

Sankey, Margaret (1997), 'The Duras Phenomenon', *Australian Journal of French Studies*, January, 34: 1, pp. 60–76.

Sayad, Cecilia (2013), *Performing Authorship: Self-Inscription and Corporeality in the Cinema*, London, New York: I. B. Tauris.

Selous, Trista (1988), *The Other Woman: Feminism and Femininity in the Work of Marguerite Duras*, New Haven, London: Yale University Press.

Shaeffer, Pierre (1946a), 'L'élément non visuel au cinéma' (1). Analyse de la 'bande son', *La revue du cinéma* 1/1, October, pp. 45–8.

—— (1946b), 'L'élément non visuel au cinéma' (2). Conception de la musique, *La revue du cinéma* 1/2, November, pp. 62–5.

Shaviro, Steven (1993), *The Cinematic Body*, Minneapolis: University of Minnesota Press.

Silverman, Kaja (1988), *The Acoustic Mirror: the Female Voice in Psychoanalysis and Cinema*, Bloomington: Indiana University Press.

Sinclair, Craig (2003), Audition: Making Sense of/in the Cinema, *The Velvet Light Trap*, Spring, 51, pp. 17–28.

Sobchack, Vivian (1982), 'Toward Inhabited Space: the Semiotic Structure of Camera Movement in the Cinema', *Semiotica*, 41, pp. 317–35.

—— (1992), *The Address of the Eye: a Phenomenology of Film Experience*, Princeton, NJ: Princeton University Press.

—— (2004), *Carnal Thoughts: Embodiment and Moving Image Culture*, Berkeley: University of California Press.

—— (2006), 'Thought on Seeing (most of) *The Descent* and *Isolation*', *Film Comment*, July–August, pp. 40–1.

Sonnenschein, David (2001), *Sound Design: the Expressive Power of Music, Voice, and Sound Effects in Cinema*, Studio City, Los Angeles: Michael Wiese Productions.

Tran, Thu Van (1976), 'Thu Van Tran', <https://thuvantran.fr/> (last accessed 1 February 2018).

Vallier, Jean (2006), *C'était Marguerite Duras*, Tome 1, 1914–45, Paris: Fayard.

—— (2010), *C'était Marguerite Duras*, Tome 2, 1945–96, Paris: Fayard.

Willis, Sharon (1987), *Marguerite Duras: Writing on the Body*, Urbana, IL: University of Illinois Press.

Filmography

Duras as director

Agatha et les lectures illimitées, film. France: Berthemont, INA, des femmes filment, 1981.

Aurélia Steiner (Melbourne), film. France: Paris Audiovisuel, 1979.

Aurélia Steiner (Vancouver), film. France: Films du Losange, 1979.

Baxter, Vera Baxter, film. France: Sunchild Production, INA, 1976.

Le Camion, film. France: Cinéma 9, Auditel, 1977.

Césarée, film. France: Films du Losange, 1979.

Des journées entières dans les arbres, film. France: Films A2, SFP Cinéma, 1976.

Détruire, dit-elle, film. France: Ancinex, Madeleine Films, 1969.

Il Dialoguo di Roma, film. Italy: Lunga Gittata RAI, 1982.

Les Enfants, film, co-directed with Jean Mascolo and Jean-Marc Turine. France: Berthemont, 1985.

La Femme du Gange, film. France: O.R.T.F., 1974.

L'Homme atlantique, film. France: Berthemont, INA, des femmes filment, 1981.

India Song, film. France: Sunchild, les Films Armorial, 1975.

Jaune le soleil, film. France: Albina Films, 1971.

Les Mains négatives, film. France: Films du Losange, 1979.

La Musica, film, co-directed with Paul Seban. France: Les films Raoul Ploquin, 1966.

Nathalie Granger, film. France: Luc Moullet et cie, 1972.

Le Navire Night, film. France: MK2, Films du Losange, 1978.

Son nom de Venise dans Calcutta désert, film. France: Cinéma 9, PIPA, Éditions Albatros, 1976.

Published film scripts

Une aussi longue absence, in collaboration with Gérard Jarlot, Paris: Gallimard, 1961.

Hiroshima mon amour, Paris: Gallimard, 1960.

Le Camion, suivi d'entretiens avec Michelle Porte, Paris: Minuit, 1977.
Nathalie Granger, suivi de *La Femme du Gange*, Paris, Gallimard, 1973.
Le Navire Night, suivi de *Césarée, Les Mains négatives, Aurélia Steiner*, Paris: Mercure de France, 1979.

Unpublished film scripts

La Bête dans la jungle, directed by Benoît Jacquot (based on Marguerite Duras' theatre adaptation *La Bête dans la jungle*, in Théâtre III, Paris: Gallimard, 1984). France: INA La Sept, 1988.
Ce que savait Morgan, directed by Luc Béraud (dialogues by Marguerite Duras). France: PI Production and O.R.T.F., 1973.
L'Itinéraire marin, directed by Jean Rollin (dialogues by Marguerite Duras and Gérard Jarlot). (The film remained unfinished). France: Les Films ABC, 1963.
Mademoiselle, directed by Tony Richardson (film script written by Marguerite Duras and Jean Genet). France, UK: Woodfall Film Production, 1966.
Moderato Cantabile, film directed by Peter Brook (script written by Marguerite Duras and Gérard Jarlot, adapted from the novel *Moderato Cantabile*, Paris: Minuit (1958)). Italy, France: Production Iena and Documento Films, 1960.
Nuit noire, Calcutta, directed by Marin Karmitz. France: MK2 Films, 1964.
Les Rideaux blancs, directed by Georges Franju. France: Régis Française de Cinéma, 1966.
La Voleuse, directed by Jean Chapot (dialogues by Marguerite Duras). France, Germany: Chronos Film Procinex and Hans Opperheimer Film, 1966.

Television

Dim, Dam, Dom, television, eight interviews conducted by Marguerite Duras. France: O.R.T.F., 1965–8.
Sans merveille, television, Michel Mitrani (film script by Marguerite Duras and Gérard Jarlot). France, shown on television on 14 April 1964.

Adaptations of Duras' own work, directed by her

Agatha et les lectures illimitées, film (adapted from her play *Agatha*, Paris: Minuit (1981)). France: Berthemont, INA, des femmes filment, 1981.

Des journées entières dans les arbres, film (adapted from her play *Des journées entières dans les arbres*, Paris: Gallimard (1968)). France, Films A2, SFP Cinéma, 1976.

Détruire, dit-elle, film (adapted from *Détruire dit-elle*, Paris: Minuit (1969)). France: Ancinex, Madeleine Films, 1969.

Les Enfants, film (adapted from her children's story *Ah! Ernesto* (1971)). France: Berthemont, 1971.

India Song, film (adapted from her play *India Song* (1973)). France: Sunchild, les Films Armorial, 1975.

Jaune le soleil, film (adapted from her novel *Abahn Sabana David*, Paris: Gallimard (1970)). France: Albina Films, 1971.

La Musica, film, co-directed with Paul Seban (adapted from her play *La Musica*, Paris: Gallimard (1965)). France: Les films Raoul Ploquin, 1966.

Adaptations of Duras' work, directed by other filmmakers

L'Amant (*The Lover*), film, directed by Jean-Jacques Annaud (adapted from the novel *L'Amant*, Paris: Minuit (1984)). France: Renn Productions and Les Films A2, 1992.

Barrage contre le Pacifique (*This Angry Age*), film, directed by René Clément (adapted from the novel *Un barrage contre le Pacifique*, Paris: Gallimard (1950)). US, Italy: Columbia Pictures Corporation, Dino De Laurentiis Cinematografica, 1958.

Un barrage contre le Pacifique, film, directed by Rithy Panh (adapted from the novel *Un barrage contre le Pacifique*, Paris: Gallimard (1950)). France: Studio 37, France 2 Catherine Dussart Production (CDP), 2008.

Dix heures et demie du soir en été (*10:30 P.M. Summer*), film, directed by Jules Dassin (adapted from the novel *Dix heures et demie du soir en été*, Paris: Gallimard (1960)). Greece, France: Jorilie and Argus Production, 1966.

La Douleur, film, directed by Emmanuel Finkiel (adapted from the novel *La Douleur*, Paris: P.O.L. (1985)). France: Les films du Poisson, Cinéfrance, 2017.

Hiroshima mon amour, film, directed by Alain Resnais. France: Argos Films, Como Films, Daiei Studio, 1959.

H Story, film, directed by Nobuhiro Suwa (a remake of Resnais's film *Hiroshima mon amour* (1959)). France and Japan: Dentsu, Imagica, 2001.

Le Marin de Gibraltar (*The Sailor from Gibraltar*), film, directed by Tony Richardson (adapted from the novel *Le Marin de Gibraltar*, Paris: Gallimard (1952)). UK: Woodfall Film Production, 1967.

Moderato Cantabile, film, directed by Peter Brook (script written by Marguerite Duras and Gérard Jarlot, adapted from the novel *Moderato Cantabile*, Paris: Minuit (1958)). France: Productions Iena, Documento Films, 1960.

Nuit noire Calcutta, film, directed by Marin Karmitz. France: MK2 Films, 1964.

Orage, film, directed by Fabrice Camoin (adapted from the novel *Dix heures et demie du soir en été* (1960)). France: Les Films du Poisson, Canal + Ciné +, 2015.

Index

Note: page numbers in *italics* indicate illustrations

Printed and bound by CPI Group (UK) Ltd, Croydon, CR0 4YY

04/02/2025

01831600-0002